SAINT GERMAIN

Studies
in
ALCHEMY

by Saint Germain
First in the Alchemy Series

published by
The Summit Lighthouse
Colorado Springs

The Summit Lighthouse, Inc.
Box A, Colorado Springs, Colorado 80901

Mark L. Prophet

The instruction set forth in *Studies in Alchemy* and *Intermediate Studies in Alchemy* was given to Mark L. Prophet by the Ascended Master Saint Germain. Under the direction of the Darjeeling Council of the Great White Brotherhood (the spiritual fraternity of saints and Ascended Beings of all ages, otherwise known as the Heavenly Hierarchy), Bishop Prophet founded The Summit Lighthouse in 1958 in Washington, D.C., to publish the teachings of the Ascended Masters. The bishop and his wife, Elizabeth Clare Prophet, were given intensive training by Saint Germain, Lord of the Seventh Ray and Hierarch of the Aquarian Age, and by the Ascended Master El Morya, Lord of the First Ray and Chief of the Darjeeling Council, in preparation for their mission to deliver the Everlasting Gospel to the age. Their book CLIMB THE HIGHEST MOUNTAIN contains a portion of that gospel in the form of instruction on cosmic law deemed by the Brotherhood as essential to mankind's transition into the Golden Age.

Mark L. Prophet made his ascension on February 26, 1973. He continues to serve the flame of God's will and to be a spokesman for Hierarchy as the Ascended Master Lanello. Elizabeth Clare Prophet was anointed as Mother of the Flame by Saint Germain, who is Knight Commander of the Keepers of the Flame Fraternity, comprised of those dedicated souls who support the cause of the Brotherhood on earth. As a representative of the Divine Mother, she nourishes the Flame of Life in the hearts of all mankind.

TABLE OF CONTENTS

Full many a glorious morning have I seen
Flatter the mountain-tops with sovereign eye,
Kissing with golden face the meadows green,
Gilding pale streams with heavenly alchemy.

Shakespeare
Sonnet XXXIII

I

The Law of Transfer of Energy

Two thousand years ago when Christ walked upon the waters of the Sea of Galilee, his demonstration was a manifestation of the natural law of levitation operating within an energy framework of cohesion, adhesion, and magnetism—the very principles which make orbital flight possible. The Light atoms composing the body of Christ absorbed at will an additional quantity of cosmic rays and spiritual substance whose kinship to physical light made his whole body Light, thereby making it as easy for him to walk upon the sea as upon dry land.

His body was purely a ray of Light shining upon the waters. The most dazzling conception of all was his ability to transfer this authority over energy to Peter through the power of Peter's own vision of the Christ in radiant, illumined manifestation. By taking his eyes temporarily from the Christ, however, Peter entered a human fear vibration and vortex which immediately densified his body, causing it to sink partially beneath the raging seas.

The comforting hand of Christ, extended in pure love, reunited the alchemical tie; and the flow of spiritual energy through his hand raised Peter once again to safety.

The further example of the Master Jesus releasing a flow of energy—as in the case of the woman who touched the hem of his garment without his knowledge aforehand— shows the impersonal love of God which responds equally to the call of faith from any of those creatures He has fashioned so wonderfully and so purely in the supreme hope of absolute cosmic freedom for all.

These two examples refer to aspects of the Great Cosmic Law which are not commonly known but which are commonly discussed or skirted about by religious groups. The law of transfer of energy is vital to the science of Alchemy; for without it, it is impossible to "create" matter. It is a law that nothing cannot create something. True knowledge of the impersonal law of transfer of energy is also vital to the correct understanding of the Great Law; for it proves that God, who makes the sun to shine on both the just and the unjust,[1] does manifest through both.

Jesus declared during his Palestinian mission that "the kingdom of heaven suffereth violence, and the violent take it by force."[2] It must be realized, then, that it is possible to wrest from the hand of God some of the secrets of governing the forces of nature and controlling matter, even though the individual and motive be not absolutely pure. But let none ever think that the one so doing shall escape from accountability; for he is fully responsible for each use or abuse of energy within his world.

The reason I am choosing to begin my exposition on Alchemy with a note of warning and a sobering explanation is not to cause anyone fear, but rather to instill in all who read a deep and abiding reverence for God—which is the only fear permitted in our octave. It is in reality holy awe that engenders within all who love the Great Law of Love the fullest respect and adoration for the wisdom which so fearfully and wonderfully made all creation in the image of fearless freedom.

All those who misuse the powers of the universe for selfish ends find sooner or later that they must relinquish their hold upon their ill-gotten gains; and the penalty they pay is frightful indeed. To produce substance to feed the poor, to heal at a touch a withered hand, to raise the dead, and even to set aside natural law and perform, by the magic of Alchemy, miracles of infinite wonder—this seems to mankind to be the ultimate in their use of Heaven's grace. Let me embrace the Spirit of freedom that makes it possible for a man made in the immortal, loving, God-free image of his Creator to do these things and many more to the benefit of society and to the happiness of his benefactors. But above all, let me praise the proper use of the blessed divine science of spiritual Alchemy.

The ancient alchemist has ever been a colorful figure—even to his own contemporaries. But time has gilded his image with a glory far greater than that which he ever possessed, and it is ever thus when approaching the aspects of mystery. It is in the simple graces of life that men will find their freedom, albeit the more complex aspects are progressive expressions of the laws of Life that shall enrich the well-being of this earth and of all its people, harnessing their total good on behalf of the most lovely world of freedom that could ever be conceived of, even in the mind of a New Atlantean!

So much for the moment regarding the world society.

Let us now consider the individual and his role in the use of Alchemy. The inner meaning of Alchemy is simply *all-composition,* implying the relation of the all of the creation to the parts which compose it. Thus Alchemy, when properly understood, deals with the conscious power of controlling mutations and transmutations within matter and energy and even within Life itself. It is the science of the mystic and it is the forte of the self-realized man who, having sought, has found himself to be one with God and is willing to play his part.

Through the years men have attempted to glamorize me with the allure of distance in time and space, which always lends enchantment to the view. I do not sell myself short as the Father's handiwork, but in common with beloved Jesus and others among the great Masters of our Brotherhood, I am especially interested that each man obtain his rightful place and the proper understanding of how he ought to exercise authority in the universe and in his own world and affairs.

Let everyone who begins this study do so with the understanding that I have a purpose in speaking here and that that purpose is to make each one of you alchemists in the truest sense of the word. This means that you must become familiar at inner levels with the all-chemistry of God and how each facet of creation is brought into manifestation in matter, in your consciousness, and in your daily life.

In order to do this properly, you will need to meditate and reread these lessons many times, calling to me and to your own God Self, your I AM Presence, for illumination on any point that is not immediately clear to you. When you have the inner degree of Alchemist of the Sacred Fire conferred upon you by your own Christ Self, you immediately become a candidate for admission to the outer court of the Great White Brotherhood.* This factor alone is a great incentive for you to become proficient in genuine spiritual Alchemy.

It has ever been a fallacy of human thought to deny the so-called miracles in the life of the great avatar Jesus. Nonetheless, he, as a son of God, revealed to all these mighty formulas which, if understood and practiced, would long ago have transformed the planet into a paradise of perfection.

Enough then of human nonsense and human creation! As Shakespeare would have said it:

Off then with the old,
The decay, and the mouldering mustiness
Of this shapeless mass:
On then with the eternal vastness
Of an unfettered spirit—
A Being of such freedom
As moving seems apart
Even from Reality
And projects the image
Of eternal hope
Into the tiniest gem or dewdrop
Cupped within a blossom rare.

I AM for the freedom of all
Lovingly,

Saint Germain

---

* The Great White Brotherhood is a spiritual order of Hierarchy, an organization of Ascended Masters united for the highest purposes of the brotherhood of man under the Fatherhood of God. The word "white" refers not to race, but to the white Light of the Christ that surrounds the saints and sages of all ages who have risen from every nation to be counted among the immortals.

II

The Purpose of Your Alchemical Experiment

Void is unfruitful energy. The alchemist must develop a sense of the value of time and space and the opportunity to manipulate both. Freedom is won by quest and conquest, but mainly by the conquest of the finite self. True mastery of the finite comes through the indrawing love, the compelling, almost magnetic heart call of the soul to its Divine Source. Only the great inflow of the cosmic Light of God can release the soul from the imprisoning shadows of its human creation. Summon then the purity of purpose which will make your creative design good; relentlessly challenge the base elements which arise like hobgoblins to disturb and try the plan you have begun; then patiently evolve your God-design—the purpose of your alchemical experiment.

The true science of the Spirit is more exact than mundane measures can yet determine. Therefore, know thy Self as the white stone or elixir from whence all thy creation must proceed in orderly fashion. If the key ideas are not created from within thee who art the alchemist, then the whole act is either hapless or an imitation of the work of another. Now if it be God thou wouldst imitate, then "Well done!" may truly be spoken of thee; but if the vanity of mankind, then piteous let thy consciousness remain. The True Self of man, from whence cometh every goodly design, is worthy to be consulted as to what it is desirable to create; therefore, the true alchemist begins his experiment by communing with himself in order to perceive the inspiring thoughts of the radiant Mind of his Creator.

It is in imitation of lesser qualities and lesser states of consciousness that society has molded many of its erroneous concepts. To correct these concepts, to forge an ennobling culture, to draw the lines of good character, man and society must look to lofty examples. Let men who would practice Alchemy learn first to mirror the great examples of all ages who have used heaven as their design; and then let them learn to select the best qualities of their lives so that Alchemy can be used as it was divinely intended, as the most noble method of achieving the desires of the heart right here and now.

I strongly suspect that many of my auditors, but few, if any, of the most sincere students, are anxious to have imparted unto them at once the philosophers' stone or the magical properties that will make them at will a combination of Aladdin and Midas with a trace of benevolence sprinkled in. I here declare for those who think thusly that while I shall impart tremendous knowledge concerning the science of Alchemy in the whole of this nine-part study, I doubt very much that unless they absorb the secrets of the first lessons with utter humility, allowing me as the instructor the privilege of preparing

7

the teachings as God would have me do, they will not at the very end find themselves wanting. And it will not be the fault of either teaching or teacher!

I do not intend to give a lengthy discourse on the vanities of worldly life; but I would like to point out that it is the hope of the Brotherhood in releasing these teachings at this time to avoid for our students the mistakes of some of the early alchemists whose sole purpose seemed to be the acquirement of riches and honor and the ability to produce from universal substance the energies to change base metals into gold. Let me hasten to say that not all of the early alchemists confined their goals to temporary gain. Indeed many stalwart souls pursued Alchemy with the same reverence they would a quest for the Holy Grail, seeing it as a divine art and the origin of the Christian mysteries as when Christ changed the water into wine at the marriage in Cana of Galilee.[1]

We desire to see the original concepts about Alchemy given new meaning, and we desire to see the meaning it acquired in the mystery schools brought to the fore. For the uses to which this science is presently put must be translated to a higher dimension if mankind are to reap the full benefits thereof. Unless this spiritual science is applied to the freeing of individuals and society from drudgery, confusion, and compromise with the densities of human thought—as is our wish—the purposes to which God ordained it will remain unfulfilled. We who pursue the high calling of the alchemist aspire to see all attain a place where they can both teach and extol the basic purposes of life to the youth of the world as having far greater than mere temporal pleasures, which in reality serve a lesser purpose to a divine alchemist than does a pacifier to a suckling child.

Let no one think because I spend this time in introducing the heart of the subject to you that my discussion is not pertinent to the facts at hand. Unless each one understands that he individually must exercise his God-given right to use power wisely and lovingly, he cannot help but fall into pits of self-delusion and rationalization.

Now it is God's plan that everyone on earth pursue the understanding of himself and his destiny. Conceit born of intellectual pride has caused many a sincere student, and even a number of worldly masters of one science or another, to fall into traps of their own creation; and in many cases they never knew when the snare was sprung. Therefore, if any subject be included here, let no one think he can omit it simply because he may seem to know it already or because he has considered it before. We place many gems of thought in the most unlikely sentences, which, though plain enough of speech and easily seen, may require more than the diligence of even an honest heart's scanning.

Saint Peter voiced the query "And if the righteous scarcely be saved, where shall the ungodly and the sinner appear?"[2] It is well for the would-be alchemist to realize that this is an exact and true science whose illumination is conferred upon man by God Himself. Its purpose is to teach mankind how to obtain for themselves every gracious gift and virtue which their lifestreams might require in finding the way back Home to God's Heart.

I do not say that you cannot learn to materialize every wish of your being—and this aspect of Alchemy is for some the easiest part of the whole, while for others it remains the most difficult. I do say that the design of those wishes ought to be contemplated more than the wondrous science of bringing them into manifestation from the invisible. For to create a worthy design is a most noble endeavor, worthy of the God in man which alone can set him free to fulfill his immortal destiny.

We have labored below and waited above for the children of this world to cease the plunder and pillage of war, to cultivate the education of the underprivileged, to relinquish the desire for class distinction, and to offer themselves as would princes of the realm to serve effectively the needs of their impoverished yet noble kin. We are presently determined to seek out the faithful of all nations and to empower them with the means whereby they can individually escape from the self-imposed bondage of the times and obtain their own priceless inheritance. Naturally, this heritage is neither temporal nor ephemeral. However, when serving in Europe to dissipate some of the poverty and confusion so prevalent there, I did use universal Alchemy to produce the substance which, although temporary in nature, supplied many human needs and was both comforting and helpful to the world and to the personal lives of my beneficiaries.

I conceive nothing wrong in the idea, nor do I look with disfavor upon your having a Divine Source of supply to meet all your needs. I do feel it is needful for you to keep constantly humble and grateful as God places within your hands the key to the control of natural forces. Again, and second to no idea contained herein, is the constant need to understand the universal scheme or plan of creation so that all that you design and do will be harmonious with eternal law and cosmic principles.

I hope that I shall have neither affrighted nor discouraged any of the students of Alchemy from pursuing this marvelous divine study. I am, however, now free to proceed with more relish; for I have magnified the eternally manifest principle of the immortal intelligence of God which some call inspiration, while others call it simply the Mind of God.

Whatever men may call a quality, it is its possession that counts the whole nine points of the Law. Therefore, love the emanation of divine wisdom contained herein, which, like sunlight shimmering through the trees, touches with its fingers of Light all through which it passes; for only by love can you truly possess.

I AM the Resurrection and the Life of cosmic purpose within you.

In the name of freedom, I remain

Saint Germain

✠

III

The Sacred Science

The domain of individual destiny is controlled by an interplay of many cosmic forces, mainly benign; but in the present world society, due to mankind's misunderstanding of both earthly and heavenly purposes, these forces have been turned to other uses, frequently chaotic and disintegrating.

Alchemy was originally intended to be a means of enriching individual destiny by making available the technique of changing base metals into gold, thereby producing opulence in the affairs of the successful practitioner. The dedication of the early alchemists to the cause of ferreting out its secrets was complete, and it was sanctified by the coordination of their minds with the works of their hands. These alchemists pursued their experiments under the duress of persecution led by the entrenched reactionary forces of their day, and it is a tribute to their lives and honor that they persisted in the search. Thus they brought forth and bequeathed to

12

humanity the bonafide results of their efforts as acknowledged scientific achievement and annotated philosophic knowledge to bless the culture and archives of the world order.

It ought to become increasingly clear to the students of this course that I am determined to bring to your minds and feelings a new sense of freedom. The wholesome concepts presented herein must indicate to your total being that the key to Alchemy that must precede the acquisition of all other keys is the mastery of yourself, to a greater or lesser degree. This key must be recognized for what it is, for self-mastery is the key to all self-knowledge. It must then be understood and used, at least in part. And you must acknowledge without question that you yourself are the alchemist who shall determine the design of your creation. Furthermore, you must know your self as the Real Self and your creation as coming forth from that Self.

It may surprise some to learn that seething vortices of humanly discordant thoughts and feelings daily impose a hypnotic effect upon almost everyone on earth. These tend to nullify the great concentration of intelligent, creative power that is the birthright of every man, woman, and child on this planet though it is consciously employed by far too few. While increasing numbers among mankind seek after freedom, the reactionary elements, either with or without purpose, attempt to burden the race with new shackles each time deliverance from one form or another of human bondage is secured.

The alchemist, to be successful, must be consciously aware of his God-given freedom to create. Those restrictions and restraints imposed upon the soul as forms of human bondage must be shunned. Yet in every case these must be distinguished from the necessary laws which structure society. Beauty and righteousness must be emblazoned upon the left and right hand to remind the would-be alchemist of his responsibility to God and man to behold his works before releasing them to see that they are indeed good, and good for all men.

I am releasing in these studies in Alchemy methods of visualization which will give to the students who will apply them as I did the ability to perform for God and man a service of the first magnitude. I trust that the myth of human equality will be dispelled and that in the dignity of equal opportunity the evolutions of this planetary home will come to know and love the expansive potential of the Christ in all. Thus the forging-ahead of humanity will be marked by a greater malleability of the soul and less ignorance of man's universal purpose to develop his individual talents than has heretofore existed on earth.

As the early alchemists attained a measure of success in probing the secrets of the universe, they became acutely aware of the need to band together and to withhold from the public eye certain discoveries which they made. A number of religious orders and secret societies grew out of this need, and the remnants thereof have survived to the present day. The need to repress as well as to express was recognized, just as enlightened men of today realize that harmony in the social order and among the nations and the eradication of the causes of war and civil strife would remove all reasons for withholding any knowledge that would prove to be universally beneficial.

Let me declare—because I can speak in the light of true knowledge—that the early alchemists were not nearly so unsuccessful as history would have men believe. Their discoveries were legion and they included knowledge both secular and religious, scientific and philosophic. Above all, they unlocked many truths which at a later date were made general knowledge.

Let not the world discount all of the stories that have been recounted of the suppression of invention and new ideas for economic and political reasons. When it suited their purposes, men in high places have ever so often instructed their hirelings to keep secret the very knowledge which belongs to the ages and which is the heritage of the people of all nations. Regardless of such dishonorable dealings, the Masters of Wisdom will never transfer this knowledge to mankind until the Alchemy of reason heals the internal breach of selfishness within enough of the race that the torch of knowledge may be everlastingly held in the selfless hand of Justice.

I am preparing your minds in these first three lessons to better assimilate the full release of wisdom's flame that has been made a part of this course. It is frequently the despair of men that they did not have a certain choice bit of knowledge long before it came into their hands. This feeling is certainly understandable, but no lamentation that is without constructive leadings is ever desirable. It is preferable that men perceive the now of the present as God's hour rather than the folded parchments of past ages. The fading hieroglyphs of yesterday's errors can neither confute the present truth nor act as a panacea to heal their unfortunate sowings; they serve only as media of contrast to amplify the present sense of gratitude that glories in such progress as now manifests to dispel the ignorance of former times.

A determined dedication to use the energies of today to open the doorway into the domain of the future is expected of the student of Alchemy. Therefore, let him see to it that his present expansion of the science of Alchemy is sufficient to transform the base qualities of the human nature into an altar on which the flame of living Reality will fire the grandeur of the Golden Age now emerging within the Christ Mind. Let his endeavors likewise be sufficient to balance the travails of world injustice; and let him work to secure for posterity eras of increasingly abundant progress, enlightenment, happiness, and universal spirituality.

When used by the alchemist, symbols and symbology properly understood are literally charged with meaning. For example, mercury is the symbol of speed and interprets to the consciousness the thought of wakeful, reverent alertness, which swiftly endows the chemistry of action with the intensity of application. Salt equates with the idea of selfhood and reminds mankind of the need to have the self retain the savor [1] of its Divine Source in preference to the crystallization of identity within the Sodom and Gomorrah of materiality indicated in the historical figure of Lot's wife. [2]

Fire, as Life, is the catalyst which can be increased from the cosmic Light within the cosmic rays in order to intensify and purify the radiance of Life in the contemplated design. Moreover, the conscious invocation of Life makes all of the alchemist's manifestations doubly secure.

Earth symbolizes the natural crystalline densities created out of Spirit's energies and sustained by the beings of the elemental kingdom. These tiny creators, in their mimicry of human discord, have transferred to nature mankind's inharmonious patterns. Thus the convergence of human error upon the planetary body came forth as thorn, thistle, insect, and beast of prey. And the Pandora's box of astral forms was opened by laggard civilizations whose misguided free will and selfishness have perverted Life's energies even on other systems of worlds. It is this discord imposed upon the very atoms of substance which the alchemist must remove from his laboratory before he can create. It is this dross which the alchemist will purify by fire.

I do not expect that every reader will immediately understand all of the concepts that are included in this course. While it is true that I advocate simplicity in the phrasing of the basic laws of God, I am also aware that thought forms worded in the higher order will be productive of greater good as the world is able to accept them. I therefore include herein elements designed to challenge those of every level of awareness to study to show themselves approved unto the God Flame within.[3] Thus individual alchemical advances will be achieved by all who faithfully apply the teachings.

The most insidious type of bondage is that in which the prisoner is not aware of his chains. I am certain that the real science of Alchemy can serve to set free everyone on earth who will accept it. Therefore, out of respect for its supreme purpose, I consider it to be the sacred science. Remember, blessed children of men, that the purpose of true science should be to increase happiness and to free the race from every outer condition that does not serve to exalt man into the pristine greatness of his original cosmic purpose.

All postulations—whether of a social, economic, religious, or scientific nature—should be infused with the freedom which allows men to progress. All who attempt to lead mankind progressively forward in these fields should admit to the possibility of change without in any way challenging those infallible pinions of the human spirit referred to as "life, liberty, and the pursuit of happiness." Certainly the opportunity for progress and the freedom to innovate cannot affect the immutability of divine Truth or the integrity of the Logos, whose power uttereth speech from those untrammeled heights to which we jointly aspire.

I AM progressively yours in the holy science,

Saint Germain

✠

IV

Dare to Do!

Versatility! I am eternally grateful for that many-splendored quality of creation! The universe is fragmented; it is spread apart from a center of oneness to a diversity of light, color, tone, and density. Each partaker of a scene, whether pastoral or of transitory ugliness, ought to remember that the splintered shafts of light rays that compose the swaddling garments of all of creation connect directly with the Great Source and Fountainhead of cosmic unity.

In my historical experiences preceding my ascension—which was identical in its raising action to the elevation of Jesus the Christ—I was in a constant state of listening grace whereby my inner ears and eyes were fixed upon a lovely realm of Light and perfection which served to remove the sting of earthly life from my consciousness, producing a comfort that my friends did not perceive. They often pondered the cause of my inner serenity without understanding its origin.

The contacts with my earthly brethren and the appearances that I have made since my ascension have not always been under circumstances where those I met were aware of either my identity or my power. May I humbly state that as in other similar cases where one of the Ascended Host has elected to part the veil of matter and maya to contact directly unascended humanity, the latter have entertained "angels unawares." [1]

I am well aware that some of my readers may opine, inasmuch as I am one who has passed through the veil, that this release of my words is of a psychic or spiritualistic nature. Let me quickly affirm that it is neither. God be praised that my own lifestream need not subscribe to such limiting forms. The fact that we are expressing or "vibrating" our Life in higher dimensions where ordinary human faculties of seeing and hearing do not function renders neither our service nor our reality of any less effect, nor does it force me to subscribe to the above-named methods of communication. Blessed ones, you do not by ordinary means perceive radio waves, for they remain inaudible until detected in the miracle of the electronic tube; therefore, trust in Heaven's capacity to communicate with man directly.

Because of my dedication to the holy cause of freedom, I have since my ascension consistently maintained a contact with one or more lifestreams embodied upon earth—and that by cosmic decree and with the approval of the heavenly Hierarchy. Beloved Jesus and other great luminaries who have descended in the fullness of the divine plan have likewise appeared to their disciples down through the ages and do occasionally manifest to men and women of today with no more effort than that employed to dial a radio or television. My purpose in discussing the subject of Heaven's winged messages from the great cloud of witnesses [2] is not as foreign to Alchemy as might at first appear; for it portrays to you a necessary part of my program in the cause of freedom, of which the current series in Alchemy is an integral part.

You see, blessed ones, the creation of the visible is wholly dependent upon those essences which are not visible to the unaided eye. Yet the central ideas occupying the minds of most people—originating as they do in the transient effects of human causation—are not of enough consequence to deserve comment or to be ordained with permanent reality. I am certain you will agree that even as the range of ordinary human experience becomes monotonous for souls both great and small, so it is a wonderful blessing to them to be able to see into the higher octaves of creation by means of an adjusted consciousness and thus draw inspiration directly from the Mind of Nature and Nature's God.

Ignorance with its defilement of the Law deprives the individual and society of enlightenment. The only cure is illumined obedience, together with scientific attentiveness to the detail of the Law. The benefits of divine wisdom remain unknown to many who suppose that the old familiar theories are adequate to meet the demands of the hour and that nothing beyond empiricism or the empirical method is required. Actually, the accepted tenets of modern science, being but partially true, are incomplete and therefore provide an inadequate foundation upon which to base advanced research and the control of the elements. An attitude of complacency does not allow for progress in any endeavor, human or divine; thus where grace might abound it does not. Complacency remains a bulwark of reactive ignorance, preventing mankind from sharing in the abundance which all Heaven stands waiting to shower upon those free souls whose purity of heart and guileless nature make most receptive to our thoughts.

Before conferring alchemical knowledge of any depth upon you, I wish to exalt you into that divine nobility which is as real as the Light of the day and your greatest strength in meeting the challenges of the morrow! To do this may require some examination of the spirit of those sincere alchemists whose excursions into the unknown were productive in more ways than one. Even the souls who failed completely to discover a method of changing base metals into gold were benefited beyond their farthest dreams by the blessings which came to them as a result of their search. Even the persecutions served to band them together in singleness of purpose, which, midst human diversity with its unfortunate tendencies toward greed and selfishness, is an achievement in itself.

I am in the hope that you will prepare yourself to succeed in your endeavors. Above all, stand ready to make the necessary changes in your thoughts and preconceived ideas that will make it possible for you to be victorious. If man expects to succeed in Alchemy, which is in truth dependent on the higher laws of spiritual science, he must nurture the faith on which the strength of his invocation and concentration will rest.

The fusion of metal, the control of atomic forces, and the direction of electronic energy by the mind of man acting in higher dimensions are easy enough once the grasp is acquired. However, after years of dependence upon the five senses and the attendant acceptance of mortal limitation, I am certain you can see how utterly important it is that your thinking become geared to new possibilities in order to function free of human restrictions and the dampening of a divine ardor by those who say because they do not know, "Impossible!" Let me say to all in freedom's name, *try!*

While you are preparing your consciousness for the reception of the knowledge of tomorrow, be aware then of the need to ponder the origin of concepts involving limitation. Beloved ones, you must be sane and balanced in all you do, but realize that true science borders on the miraculous to those who do not understand its formulas. You approach a solid wall with the idea that you cannot walk through it; yet it is not solid at all, but as full of holes as the wire of a chicken coop. You cannot walk upon hot coals without burning your feet, and yet medicine men of a less illumined culture than your own do so with impunity.

Countless miracles of Christ have been duplicated by men and women of various times and climes since His wondrous advent; and yet because of human skepticism and forgetfulness, the wonder of it all has been relegated to the realm of myth or the imaginings of gullible minds. Let me plead for a renewal of faith in the power of God, for this is a requirement of everyone who would be a wonder man of spiritual accomplishment on behalf of the holy purposes of the Universal Law itself.

Without faith it is not only impossible to please God,[3] but I declare unto you, it is impossible to manifest the perfection of His laws. As faith is so great a requirement, would it not pay well for each one to reexamine his reasons for doubt? Note well that most doubts arise from patterns of self-deception and the practice of deceit and the failures of the human mind to fulfill its professed integrity. Seeing then that such negative conditions stem from the consciousness of error, would it not be ever so wise for all to look unto Me (the Presence of Almighty God) and live? [4]

With God all things are possible; [5] but as in every science, proficiency does not usually come about without knowledge and its persistent application. The few who are exceptions to this rule may be called geniuses; but when the whole Law is understood, it will be proven that even they had their hours of diligent study and practice.

I particularly want to point out that the purpose of our release of alchemical secrets in this course is to place in your hands and in the laboratory of your consciousness the knowledge of the Law which we ourselves have used for centuries with the greatest of success and with the reverence for Life which is of prime necessity to an inquiring mind poised on the loving intent of an honest heart. Here idle curiosity is exchanged for that moral grandeur which so lifts a man above his fellows as to make of him a divine star in the firmament of his contemporaries. Lifted then by no false pride or intellectual misinterpretations, the true alchemist stands with humble mien, gazing expectantly at the teacher who will impart to him, if the attitude and the application be correct, the priceless knowledge of the ages.

May I fondly hope that you will reread the early lessons and assimilate therefrom a new sense of progress and of new possibilities? I am determined that many in this class shall succeed; and I shall continue to do my part above and below in your octave that this prove true and that great illumination, hope, peace, and understanding be born and renewed within you all.

I AM faithfully yours,

Saint Germain

V

The Need, Power, and Motive of Change

The now of the present hour must be utilized as a chalice of spiritual opportunity. Life must be indulged by its highest objectives, honored by the adoration of exalting principles, and merited by selfless service. Beloved people, the power to change is within every man. Prefer this power and venerate it above every limiting condition, and watch the Alchemy of Self expand!

Transmute the lies of shadowed substance that arrest your spirit's upward soaring. Realize that conditions of human limitation are but ghosts that parade upon the stage of mortal existence, only to be laid to rest forever by eternal Reality. Each man must become aware of his choices and select either freedom or fetters as he explores the chemistry of his present state, brings it into focus upon the mirror of truth, and then determines to alter each base condition, constructing within the crucible of the hour that hallowed progress which is born of eternal perception.

Destruct, then, the base and senseless mania of your

origin in matter consciousness, that possessive nature, the perversion of the Mother, which, failing to assess the fullness of cosmic possibilities, limits itself to the baubles and trinkets of temporal possession. Let Heaven use your consciousness to expand its window into the infinite, and then behold at last the beautiful possibilities present in the most dire outer conditions. Give wealth to the poor in spirit, understanding to the rich, and compassion to everyone.

So often a lifestream may have in abundance the very qualities in which his neighbor is lacking. Exchange your virtues by exalting the valleys of another, and trust Life to remove the peaks of his pride as well as your own. Transmute the conditions in your own world that you do not want by determined and persistent effort. Every Divine Being who exalts the life of God within you knows that the power to do these things is in your hands this very day, within the reach of your intelligence and spirit.

Construct those spires of attainment which compose the Celestial City, and enfold the world of physical substance, the conscious mind, and the feelings of your heart with the radiance of immortal spheres. Gazing at the universe with renewed hope, behold the need to sustain the proper regard. Vanity has held sway upon earth far too long. Wondrous opportunities, like spirits in the night, have vanished with the dawn, resisted by the cold shackles that imprison the soul in a mantle of disintegrating moments descending in the glass of the hours.

The son of Elizabeth inquired of the Christ, "Art thou He that should come or look we for another?"[1] The reply of the Christ referred to His miraculous accomplishments: the deaf were made to hear, the blind to see, and the lame to walk. The lesson contained in His answer urges each lifestream to accept the greatness of his own Reality. All should see that Life has brought to them its great and wondrous graces through the "I AM He" consciousness which must emerge from the cave of materiality. The gross separation of the whole into weak and incomplete components—men's concept of themselves as particles remote from their Source—obliges their struggle through human misfortune instead of their acceptance of the grandiose concept of cooperative oneness charged with the power of love and freedom unbounded.

Truth raises all and defeats no one save those enemies of righteousness whose shadowed misunderstanding makes them little more than savage animals in the jungle of human creation. Even these are given more compassion by Life than they deserve; this I know, because the record is laid before me. Beloved Kwan Yin has called for mercy and given it freely to all without limit and without price. This is God's great gift: He always returns more love to life than life ever gives to Him. Selflessly, the magnitude of God sends forth a torrent of love when a few droplets would suffice and thereby sweeps mankind on the upward pilgrim way, regardless of men's erroneous notions.

Now, looking to another is not the solution to your problems; nor will it win the intended fulfillment God holds for thee, blessed son of man. As an alchemist enlightened by the torch of divine knowledge, aware of the magnificence of true Selfhood, you must summon the strength from the invisible realm and use the processes of transmutative Alchemy within your own world and affairs to master daily all outer conditions by the spiritual means and physical appurtenances available to you. To make bricks without straw ² may not always be a requirement

27

and may seem most difficult, but to the determined alchemist it is merely an obstacle to be overcome.

No one who occupies the earth at present should limit his recognition of the now-is-the-hour concept which mounts each wave of opposition and rides it forward into the crest of victory. Everyone should see his life—at any age or time—as amenable to change for the better and himself as possessing the capability to surmount any condition at will. Law and justice are natural factors of control; but the universe, guided by its own law, has the creative methods of transcending that law, approximating cosmic dimensions, and expanding geometrically into infinity.

Friends of freedom must disallow old ideas as quickly as they are able and discard outworn concepts as outmoded garments. It was difficult for men to accept that the world was round in Columbus' day; they dogmatically subscribed to the theory that the earth was flat. Chemical formulas of basic and complex matter are simple to the chemist but to the unlearned seem but a jumble of symbols.

Our purpose in this course is not merely to confer knowledge, but to effect your acceptance of that knowledge by an almost a priori methodology. This is needed because the categorical proof of alchemical laws is universally and necessarily seen through their action in man! Let there be Light within your personal orbit and within the sphere of your being. Life is not an experiment, but mankind have experimented with it. Humanity has ridden the tide of the peripheral world of effects while neglecting the inner causative realm. All unhappiness is rooted in basic factors of cause. Mend the flaws and you shall be self-healed and self-revealed.

I am interested in bringing about a complete reversal of deleterious human attitudes and replacing them by such right methods and concepts that each life can quickly rise out of the human forcefield with its heavy, gravitational magnetism that hinders mankind's progressive ascension. By transmutation let every would-be alchemist first act to transform himself here and now, and gain thereby an inner peace and a sense of outer accomplishment— especially at the close of each life's term. Surely, unless both an interior and an exterior focus be maintained where Good is accented, one's concentration of positive control which has the power to alter substance within and without cannot manifest the blessing God intends all to have and exercise each day.

Beloved ones, a life lived for reward or punishment is not a raison d'être. The destiny inherent within life has escaped the intelligent comprehension of many on earth and is anchored in but a few. Thousands daily take pleasure in the sweepstakes, the races, or games of chance, hoping against fantastic odds to become a winner, whilst they ignore the most certain of all laws: the cosmic purpose.

Those who deny God or Life itself do so out of a dearth of genuine experience. They have not witnessed the dawn of pure reason in themselves. They prefer to accept those popular ideas associated with "non-gullibility!" Well, the losses of such as these are legion; and while I do not expect to change every such individual, I do repeat my admonishment here that all might be inspired to keep on keeping on. The search is worth all effort. I know the Law; the Alchemy of action is its own proof.

Those who desire to enter into debate to prove the nonexistence or the nonessentiality of a First Cause may not wish to lose the transient pleasure of so doing; but if they accede to the divine logic, the golden grain of Truth will replace the husks of pride in the stifling, airtight systems of the human intellect which disdains the verification of any knowledge not experienced by the physical senses.

Frequently individuals like to think they are *en rapport* with hoary heads of wisdom. Now I think that the centuries I lived before my ascension and those which have since transpired have entitled me to some distinction in this respect. Neither ego nor human motive would inspire me to write this series. I am aware only of the deep love I feel for the earth as a unit of cosmic progress, and I desire to impart herein something of the sweet simplicity of that love and the wisdom that is guided thereby.

Let us see now how reasonable it is to suppose that enough people serving in harmony can change the most calcified condition and create an influx of love that will sweep the hills and valleys with an inspired movement to heal the breach between the realities of eternal Alchemy (the All-chemistry of God) and the artificialities which rise from the caves of base error. Then the emerging gold of personal integrity and personal integration will be a gift equally shared by all; individual man will reflect pure genius and the social order will reflect the kingdom of heaven. The forces that would bind mankind to their past errors and thus prevent the flame of peace from being released in the present must themselves be bound as in heaven, so on earth. And mankind must arise to sound the death knell of these forces here and now ere war shall cease. Freedom from confusion can be found only in the true understanding of Life and the Alchemy of Being.

Step by step, I am leading you to the right

understanding of Alchemy. In the first lessons I reminded you of responsibility—your responsibility to prove the law of your Being by the right use of Alchemy. Now I am reminding you of the need to effect changes in yourself where change is desirable. Finally, I shall instruct you in the art and practice of precipitation. A prerequisite to applying the methods of precipitation is knowing what you want to precipitate. It was this truth which Jesus taught in the Lord's Prayer and when he said, "Nevertheless, not my will, but Thine be done." [3]

The will of God, the will of the Higher, is the will of your Real Self—the most important part of you. Because the lesser you, although it retains through the soul the capacity to contact this Higher Self, is but a bundle of impulses crowded with bits of human knowledge, I am advocating that you become acquainted with the Reality of yourself; for this Reality is the genie (genius) in you that can give the Aladdin (symbolizing the alchemist who rubs the lamp of pure knowledge) the right desires of his Immortal Being.

Ponder now the need to change (Thine is the kingdom), the power to change (Thine is the power), and the motive to change (Thine is the glory), and evolve out of the passing flame of earnestness the permanent sun of renewed hope.

Graciously, I AM

Saint Germain

✠

VI

Molding Factors

Ah, the mold—there's the rub! Aye, and the mowlde,* too, contaminates!

But how beautiful is the original hope of Heaven for each lifestream! Following the descent into form and material substance come those formative years when the pressures, both clamorous and silent, make their impression upon the clean white consciousness of the individual. Beginning with the first fond gawking of parents and kin, there is a gradual build-up of environmental factors which serve to create patterns and concepts upon the tender screen of the embryonic mind.

These molding factors continue to exert their multifarious influence upon the plastic personality of man. That selfhood, then, which is first identified wholly with God-Good is affected and shaped by myriad experience patterns. Thus does example, for woe or for weal, sculpt the mind and being of man. Experience is not, however,

* Middle English for mold.

32

the sole way to expand consciousness; for each moment spent with God or one of His cosmic band serves to exalt and broaden individual consciousness, conveying illumination on the instant—in the twinkling of an eye!

The empirical proof of human imperfection is epitomized in the past-present lives of mass humanity. Life in bondage and life in peril decries the meaning of existence. Religion and hope for salvation arise in the human heart and burgeon from the human tree! ("And he looked up and said, I see men as trees walking.")[1] The alchemy of change was needed in Jesus' day and is still needed, because all too frequently the mold is imperfect and the product cannot excel its matrix.

I have declared that the mowlde, too, contaminates; and thus I direct your attention to the untransmuted accumulation of human filth and misery which, like trash, litters the sidewalks of the human consciousness, reeking forth from the literary stalls of the world. The crusty mowlde masquerades as legitimate culture while undermining the decency of lusty souls. Freedom of the press was not intended to give license to the corrupters of youthful minds; neither was it intended to be used to confuse and disorganize the populace, flooding their brains with jingoistic propaganda and prejudicial dis-criminations. Rather, the power of Light was intended to emanate from a free press and exalt everyone into a rightful sense of cosmic destiny.

America, my beloved country! How precious are the footsteps of your heroes sung and unsung; but every mother's heart can take a just pride in offering with the "consent of the governed" the fruit of her life—sons and daughters of excellence who from the heart of this beloved nation serve the cause of freedom across the earth.

Because each dire effect of the mold and the mowlde must be counteracted, I am releasing these remarks pertaining to personal freedom through the correct use of Alchemy. I do not say that more will not be spoken on the subject to parallel and conclude the course, but herein is my specific advice to those who would use Alchemy to further their own personal advancement in the divine plan fulfilled and thus change their present circumstances for the better.

Those who are familiar with the process of refining precious metals are aware of the intense heat needed to liquify many metals. Heat is also necessary to release impurities and foreign material from the pure metal. Separation of the dross occurs in two ways: (1) a portion is vaporized and passes into the very atmosphere of the room wherein the refining furnace is operating, and (2) much of this unwanted substance is brought to the surface and skimmed off by the alert refiner.

Apropos of this, few parents exist who are equipped with the type of instruction which would enable their children to know from the beginning the tenets of their full freedom. I do not say that the world is not full of aspiration and good intentions, but the highways so paved do not seem to lead to the best places. Thus it happens that the children of the world become wiser in each succeeding generation in the arts and artifices of war and in the many customs of world society without ever becoming too stirred about the regenerate and peaceful society of saints!

In the main, few are born and come to years with a right understanding of the universal purpose; and of necessity, personal destinies, which often run crosscurrent to the universal flow, are periodically thwarted and broken. The pages of history are full of the downfall of tyrants and the overthrow of monsters of misdirected purpose. Failures and successes in many fields draw recognition while the average man moves into the burial ground of mediocrity. Nothing is further from the plan of God and Nature than these counterfeits of the golden mean.

How ill-equipped is the concept of a destiny which can be shaped by human misconceptions. How noble are they who acknowledge an Intellect, a Mind, a Spiritual Overseer, and a Creator whose forethought, greater even than that of His emissaries, is revealed as a mountain of universal purpose to be scaled by the brave who do not hesitate or fear to trust the wisdom of those early climbers of the rugged summit peaks.

Those linked to the lifeline of these spiritual pioneers are given greater guidance, for the Elder Brothers of the race lovingly extend to them the freedom of the ages as a gift of faith. This gift is extended to all who, by accepting that faith, can likewise summon the will to pursue it and the perseverance to let it fashion them in a mold made purer still and in an accumulation of that purity whose reality is the treasure of heaven!

Beloved friends of freedom, you stand now at the gateway to higher alchemical truths, which I am releasing in the seventh lesson; but it is needful for you to contemplate your life in a manner wholly in keeping with the Spirit of universal Alchemy. No longer act from the vanity of desiring recognition, but from the valor of necessary achievement and because service is needed and worthy in itself. God needs a vehicle through which to manifest in the world of form, and you lend your hands and feet to Him! You must understand the mystery of Oneness whereby a thread of contact between each life and its Source serves to connect all who live to one great central switchboard. Here the interaction of thought and feeling is guarded lest it hurt any part of Life in the holy mountain of God.

Consider all the beauty of life which can be. Perceive this as pure gold. All causes of unhappiness, every vibration of discord, fear, doubt, suspicion, condemnation, criticism, judgment, self-righteousness, and all negative traits are part of either the human mold or the mowlde which must be purged as dross before purity can so regenerate a lifestream as to enable the individual to partake of the waters of Life freely.[2]

It is not enough that men come to drink when the invitation from Higher Sources has gone forth. They must make new skins to retain the new wine of infinite goodness and purpose.[3] This is spiritual Alchemy; and wise are they who first master it in themselves before attempting to govern the elements in others or in nature, for thus is karma justified by wisdom and rendered benign. Sin does not come to the door of such a practitioner; for his motives, purposes, and methods are pure, and his acts are also just.

Gracious alchemists, the very fact that you are studying this course should denote your interest in improving. In the very word *improving* is a spiritual lesson to be mastered. The words *impression* and *proving* combine here to denote that Life brings its impressions to the heart of your consciousness to prove the worth of each impression. Every idle thought is thereby brought to judgment before the magnificence that is the higher glory of God, the upper Light in the vaulted chamber of heaven.

The Mind of Christ is synonymous with the Mind of

Light and characterizes one whose attunement is specifically directed to the Higher Intelligence. The inflow of impressions from the world at large should be directed by the student for comparison and proof to the pure patterns of the purposes of Heaven. When these are improved upon by the alchemical fire, they become part of each man's forte of useful objects and ideas—permanent matrices for good, drawing unto the consciousness of man more of their kind. Thus is the kingdom of Selfhood expanded on wings of heavenly wisdom proved day after day by the speech uttered from the hills of spiritual watchfulness.

The sincere alchemist knows that the vast Intelligence that created all that is, expands mighty wings of Light over the all of the Cosmos. As above in the Macrocosm, so below in the microcosm, in the miniaturized world of appearance, is this Intelligence individualized! The watchful care of God ever manifests to His wondrous purposes as a Guardian Presence who seeks not the defilement, but the glorious fulfillment of each person in whom dwells the Flame of almighty, ever-present Life.

So-called physical death does not represent the end of being. It merely divides eternal Life into compartments of identity and experience whereby expansion and opportunity can be utilized to the fullest and each outworn mold discarded. Forgotten fragments can be pieced together by the seeker and woven strand by strand into a tapestry of such beauty as to thrill the beholder with a sense of gratitude for the perfection and glory present in each day of eternity!

I am aware of human discouragement caused by identifying with elements of disintegration in society. I know full well the deceits practiced in the name of religion; but my concern is not so much with these matters as it is with those lives that do emerge from the crucible of experience with a wonderful garment patined with pure gold.

Your life need never be vacant, for Life watches you and Life is intelligent and considerate. Life is tangible and real. Life is earnest and tender. Life is dramatic and moving toward glory. The high road, as distinguished from the low road, is the way of the alchemist, whose heart is in the shining glory all the day and all the way that his pilgrim feet walk the dusty ways of man, transmuting, transmuting, and transmuting that dust into purest radiance!

I AM the Life, I AM the Truth, and I AM the Way,

Saint Germain

✠

VII

Methods of Transfer

Light is the alchemical key! The words "Let there be Light"[1] are the first fiat of the creation and the first step in proper precipitation. When man, who himself is a manifestation of God, desires to emulate the Supreme Father and precipitate, as a true son of Light should learn to do, he ought to follow those methods used by the Supreme Intelligence if consistent and worthy results are to be anticipated.

By examining the obvious methods of the Creator and by observing nature, you can deduce much of value if you will school yourself to think independently. For it is necessary to bypass mere human syllogisms and to penetrate the limitless Consciousness of God, who is the great Master Alchemist, in order to "go and do likewise,"[2] ever beholding your services as good.

When you have determined within yourself to experiment with the art of precipitation, first create a mind blueprint of the object you wish to produce. This should incorporate definite size, proportion, substance, density, color, and quality in detailed picture form. When the visualization of the blueprint within your mind is complete, it ought to be immediately sealed; this is a vital step in its speedy and effective release into the world of Matter-form.

Do not misunderstand this step and think that by sealing your plan you are closing the door to the improvement of its design. Such is not the case, for improvements can be made in subsequent models; but unless you release the blueprint to the elementals and builders of form as a finished work, they cannot properly bring it into manifestation. The words "It is finished!" are therefore the second fiat of creation following "Let there be Light!"

Now that you have created a thought matrix and sealed it against the intrusion of impinging mind radiation from others, set up either consciously (in some cases through jealousy or ego) or unconsciously by the mass mind's collective resistance to progress, you must observe the third rule to protect your creative intent and "tell no man." This, too, is a law of precipitation—one that allows you to circumvent concentrated beams of human thought and feeling patterns which can be most disturbing to a successful alchemical experiment unless certain safeguards are activated.

Avoid, then, the dissipation of energy by the intrusion of a multiplicity of minds, except where two or more individuals are specifically cooperating in joint precipitation. Those who are of a scientific nature and are familiar with coulomb scattering and Rutherford's law will understand how thought-energy, as waves scattering other waves, as if composed of minute particles, can set up a penetration of great enough intensity to break down the field of magnetic thought-energy focusing the specific pattern of the creative matrix.

Each student should recognize that geometric figures, such as the square, the triangle, the circle, the ellipse, and the parallelogram, are employed almost universally in creating within the macrocosmic as well as the microcosmic three-dimensional world. Although higher forms of creativity are found in the mathematical world of algebra, calculus, and trigonometry, the highest symbology of all known to us at inner spiritual levels is the science of engrammic rhythms. This study deals with the control and release of energy, with engrams (which term we use to refer to the causative key behind the effects observed by worldly scientists and called by them engrams), with the use of mantras, with the storing of fohatic energy, and with safeguards activating principles of demarcation between the evolutions of the human consciousness in the planes of Matter and the world of perfect divine order that exists in the planes of Spirit.

When contemplating this science, one should bear in mind that even the infinite, omnipresent Consciousness of God, as it extends itself into the realm of the material creation, moves through the gamut of creative expression from simple patterns to those of increasing complexity.

The student of Alchemy should consider the memory, when employed as the instrument of the Higher Mind, as an invaluable adjunct to his experiment; for the processes of the human memory are remarkable indeed. And when these are coordinated with the mental body, superlative action is always forthcoming. Thus there are a number of individuals who can memorize and execute an entire symphony without noticeable flaw. Mathematicians, too, demonstrate marvelous faculties of mental control in their calculations which approximate infinite precision. Let each student of Alchemy, then, recognize that he has within himself a Higher Mind that is capable of holding patterns of infinite dimensions. This Mind functions independently of the outer mind without human restriction of any kind. Hence, as the vehicle of the Higher Mind, a purified memory body, feeding as it does the impressions of that Mind to the outer mind, is indispensable to the alchemist.

Let the sincere student who would ponder and practice methods of mind and memory control, which are the methods of God Himself, acquire the habit of consciously giving to this blessed Higher Mind, or Christ Self, the responsibility for designing and perfecting the embryonic ideas and patterns of his creation. For many of these patterns which at first appear to be consciously conceived by the alchemist frequently have their origin within this higher portion of the blessed self. Remember, twenty-four hours of each day your Higher Mind is active in expanded dimensions. This blessed Comforter, unknown and unexperienced by you outwardly, waits to be called into action and does function free of ordinary space-time limitations. Employ your Higher Mind, then, both as your apprentice and as your teacher; for the Holy Spirit of Truth moving therein can lead you into all truth!

I would like to call to the attention of the students that if they so desire, they can immeasurably assist themselves in the alchemical arts through outside reading. Care must be exercised in this, however, so that the byways of technology and scientific theory do not serve to divert the mighty flow of Alchemy as the greatest science into byways of materialism where the ends are said to justify the means. I realize full well that many related subjects would not only be boring, but also beyond the comprehension of some of our students. Desiring not to limit the masses of mankind from having the blessings of Alchemy, I have deliberately stated many of these points in such a way as to make them easily understood. Let no one feel, however, that all knowledge can be reached through a single approach or without effort and study.

I suggest for those wishing more technical information to augment the course that they study wave propagation, the mechanics of the quantum theory, elementary and advanced chemistry and physics, seismology, astronomy, geology, and related subjects. These studies, together with courses in the humanities, the world's religions, and the Shakespearean plays, will be of immense value as you are guided from within and also by your personal tastes. Let none feel that the pursuit of such extracurricular subjects is absolutely necessary or the mandate of the Masters; for the teachings of greatest importance are included herein—albeit in some cases between the lines. Let God guide; and to those who do not recognize His reins, I say, fortune is as fortune does!

I am a bit hopeful that material science will not look too much askance on the control of matter by the power of the mind and spirit. I doubt that religion could justly deny the so-called miracles which demonstrate (if they are to be believed) that individuals who have lived upon earth have been able to practice transmutation, which is simply changing one form into another, such as water into wine;[3] amplification and multiplication of the atomic and molecular substance, such as multiplying the loaves and fishes;[4] and precipitation of the elements, such as calling down fire from heaven.[5] Equally wondrous feats performed by Masters unascended and ascended indicate a most exact science of control over matter and energy.

I myself have never questioned the truth of these matters, simply because I have always retained in humility my faith in the power of Good to endure forever; moreover, I am active in demonstrating the laws of Alchemy which make of the entire process of the control of matter and energy an everyday affair. I realize that the uninitiated or those who have never seen these so-called miracles for themselves may easily question their authenticity. Alchemists of God, I do not now ask you to believe alone. I ask you to begin in some measure to demonstrate these truths for yourself!

A few students of higher law have been able to externalize successfully one or more visible objects directly from the Universal such as a rose, a precious stone, or a cup of liquid essence quickening both mind and body. Naturally, we are anxious to see people achieve the power of producing anything and everything directly from the Universal. Yet such secrets can hardly be written down or spelled out in full, for we cannot upset the present economic system until greater justice is established by mankind on earth; but neither can these secrets be justifiably concealed from the worthy. Hence we have included marvelous keys in this total course which, to the eyes of the faithful or those who would strive to become so, will open many a door of progress.

Every Ascended Master has these powers to precipitate at will, and therefore he never lacks for any good thing. Let unascended mankind ask themselves this question: How long will you spend your energy struggling to eke out a bare existence from Nature's cupboard, which to some seems bare indeed, when all your needs can be met by mastering the cosmic laws which Christ Jesus and other great teachers have demonstrated by their own lives in the past?

The use of the term "light" in Alchemy includes light in its known visible aspects as well as in its invisible characteristics, some of which are yet unknown to physical science. When I produced rare gems and precious stones by means of Alchemy, the methods I used could not have been easily applied by the average person who had not by discipline, faith, and meditative quietude established the necessary mind control.

These methods are known to every initiate; and only an initiate could be so tempted of the dark forces as Jesus was, who, aware of his alchemical power, rebuked the temptation to use Alchemy during the period of the testing of his faith. Rather than relieve physical discomfort by commanding "these stones be made bread,"[6] as he might have done, he rendered his allegiance to the supreme God Presence and the Word of God and acknowledged these as far more important than the demands of his physical body. This enabled him to pass his test and to prepare for the disciplines which gave him his victory on the cross and in the tomb and carried him upward from Bethany's hill into the arms of God.

However, the Alchemy of spiritual progress seems less important to many who prefer the more spectacular modes of psychic phenomena to the attainment of those transmutative changes which will make them godlike. Little do men dream that the assurance "All these things shall be added unto you"[7] includes the power of control over wind and wave, of substance and energy, once man has made the kingdom of God his first and most important objective. However, balance is needed; and I am delighted once again to tell the students that the use of Alchemy to work change in the physical octave is not inordinate in the least if it is properly used.

The methods of Alchemy can be simply stated and easily absorbed, but its precepts require the practice of a master artist. Nevertheless, results can come forth in diverse ways if the student will at least begin and try. There are many methods of precipitation, but here I shall outline just one of them in part.

First design a mental matrix of the desired object; then determine where you wish it to manifest. If you know the material substance of which it is composed, memorize its atomic pattern; if not, call to the Divine Intelligence within your Higher Mind to register the pattern for you from the Universal Intelligence and impress it upon your memory body and your mind.

Recognize that light is an energy substance universally manifesting on earth, thanks to the sun-center of Being, the focal point of the Christ in this solar system. Call for light to take on the atomic pattern you are holding, to coalesce around that pattern, and then to "densify" into form. Call for the multiplication of this atomic structure until molecules of substance begin to fill the void occupying the space in which you desire the object to appear. When the total outline is filled with the vibratory action of the fourth-dimensional substance representing the desired manifestation, ask for the full lowering of the atomic density into three-dimensional form and substance within the pattern established by the matrix of your mind; and then await results.

Do not be tense if your manifestation is not immediate or if after a reasonable length of time it appears that results are not forthcoming. Remember, blessed ones, despair destroys the very faith upon which your experiment is built; for faith is the substance of things hoped for, the evidence of things not seen, [8] and you must hold your faith as you hold the gossamer veil composing the mental image. If you have spent years in the grip of human emotions absorbing the discord of the mass consciousness and the doubts and fears of humankind, these records must be consumed by alchemical fires to make way for these nobler ideas and forms which you would image forth. To your new ideas you must give your time and your energy. Thus you begin to weave a web of fruition dedicated to spirituality, to the spiritualization of the material consciousness, and to the materialization of heavenly concepts right here on earth where the kingdom of God must come into manifestation.

I would like to point out that the scanning method used in the projection of television pictures, whereby an electronic stream effect fluoresces on a screen and the electronic particles sweep in a horizontal linear pattern to create within a microsecond an eye picture, cannot be successfully used in alchemical precipitation, but is most suitable for the projection of mental pictures at a distance. In precipitation, a rapid expansion of the light rays in three dimensions must occur; and in the screen method, the optical image is on a flat, single-plane dimension.

A study of cytology and embryology will provide the student with some understanding of how a single cell multiplies and reproduces. When you are dealing with instantaneous manifestation, the velocity and intensity of Light must reach startling speed and power. It must be realized that the exercise of such control over matter by the mind is no ordinary process. While I do not say that ordinary people cannot master the technique of executing these laws and that the most humble individual cannot be invested with or invest himself with such authority within the inalienable rights that God gives to man, I do not wish a sense of frustration to arise within those who may attempt to precipitate and then feel discouraged because they apparently fail.

I say "apparently" because the Law does not fail. In most cases where direct precipitation does not occur, if the effort and the technique be pursued in full faith that the call compels the answer, an indirect precipitation will sooner or later be brought about whereby through one hand or another the desired manifestation does take place. Remember, this is divine artistry of the highest type; it is also co-creation with God and, as such, is best used by those whose purposes parallel the divine. Thus when the will of man is aligned with the will of God, the Light of God does not fail to precipitate that will in the fullness of time, space, and opportunity.

I have devoted six lessons to this subject, dealing with practical methods for assisting the spiritual scientist in obtaining greater personal happiness each day through the merger of the person with the patterns of Principle itself. Both inner and outer peace and a sense of personal well-being are required for the successful development of one's spiritual powers, albeit some individuals may thrive in the midst of conflict. I admit that upon earth courageous leaders in many fields are needed to unfold and develop the type of society which could be considered to be designed by the gods. In addition to the Alchemy of instantaneous precipitation, the Alchemy of preparation is needed, whereby the use of one's energies and opportunities is planned in an intelligent manner so that Life does not receive a hit-and-miss return on its investment of energy in an individual lifestream.

I am hopeful that my readers thus far have not been disappointed in the homey use I have made of their time and attention. I humbly submit that the rereading of this material may further enlighten you, each one, in the true depth of my perceptions, which are calculated to exalt those of various social and religious strata into areas of greater usefulness to themselves, to mankind, and to God. If, when the course is complete, I have in some measure accomplished that or augmented its possibility, I shall be content.

Some of you may desire my personal guidance as you attempt your first alchemical precipitation. I shall gladly assist all who will silently request my aid, providing the motive be right and the desired change beneficial to your life plan and providing you exercise care and prayer in seeking that God's will always be done. Let me suggest, then, that you attempt as a first effort the precipitation of an amethyst in the form of a Maltese cross. You see, this would be most excellent; for I have personally used Alchemy to make many experimental models. And I am most happy to add my momentum to your own!

From the simple to the complex, from the dawn of the beginning of the use of Light's ray to the noontide zenith of progress, let all move in the byways of life as in a caravan of faith. Let each would-be alchemist aim at the mark of achievement. You build in the eternal day right now.

I AM dedicated to your success,

VIII

Commanding Consciousness

Now we approach with reverent hush, with the awe of sacred awareness, the great spiritual laws governing all outer manifestation. The purposes of God become more near to each one as they become more dear to Him. Realize what folly it is to submit to the false tenets of any educational system; yet it is equally foolish to deny the inherent truth and the tested precepts of academic knowledge.

To know nature, know thyself; but master the art of sacred synthesis. Thereby the justice of truth shall serve to integrate within the field of knowing that inner relativity and cosmic measurement between nature and the Self whose precise mathematical action indicates that as God geometrizes, so man is able systematically to perceive and demonstrate a correlated understanding of the wondrous works of God's hands—minus the fallacious wizardry of the carnal mind.

By stripping human thought and feeling vibrations

50

from the creative grace enfolded within each atom of the creation, the whole substance of Life gleams, purified by eternal hands. Now this is as it should be! The grossest error, the most intense suffering—all are caused by an erroneous approach to pure reason. Do you realize, blessed children of mankind, that few there be upon earth who would knowingly persist in wrong doing were they convinced with certainty that they were so engaged? It is up to the master alchemists of the race, then, to serve God and man to the ultimate by removing every trace of malice and ignorance from the screen of the human consciousness, commencing with each one's own personal concepts.

Knowing how tenderly the students of this course are hanging on my every word, I am also imbued with a sense of reverence for the service at hand. I cannot conceive of how we can do less than answer the calls made unto us in accordance with the Great Cosmic Law. Even an Ascended Being in close contact with mankind can become almost possessed with a sense of urgency and a desire to cut the chains which hold any blessed soul in bondage! Yet it is only possible for us to point the way and give such specific guidance and service as the Karmic Board* has prescribed.

The injunction "Man, know thyself" must be applied by you to the pure truth of Being and not to human concepts of what that truth is. It is dangerous, however, to be critical of another or of his concepts; for only the individual can apprehend, through the screen of his own being, his world and the Cosmos beyond. When you realize the meaning of interpreting life for yourself, you will see how utterly impossible it is for you to perform this for another, inasmuch as the average person cannot successfully enter the consciousness of another lifestream

* The board of spiritual overseers who represent the Godhead in administering justice to mankind.

nor accurately assess his complete thought and feeling processes.

This, by the grace of God, we are able to do; and the Karmic Board, in connection with the universally Christed Selves of all mankind, is able to mediate. We often hesitate, unless mightily appealed to, to interfere in individual karma; yet foolish unascended mankind often rush in to decide how an individual ought to live or think. I trust the students of this activity will come more and more to realize how helpful they can be to one another by holding the immaculate concept for each one's life plan and then leaving the guidance to that one's Higher Self.

Well have I observed over the centuries how important is the service of ordered prayer. The daily offering of petitions has saved the lives of millions, expanded the lives of other millions, and blessed all Life without limit. Prayer opens the door of God's intervention in human affairs. It provides an avenue whereby the Ascended Masters and Cosmic Beings who desire to serve the planet earth and its evolutions can walk within the folds of universal justice and render special assistance because they have been called upon to do so. For the Law decrees that the heavenly hosts must be petitioned by some among mankind, must be invited to intervene, before they are permitted to intercede on behalf of humanity.

After all, would men retain their free will if Heaven thwarted the attainment of every inordinate desire? Yet can those guardians of the race who perceive the error of mankind's actions fail to invoke on behalf of their misguided brethren assistance from the higher intelligence of God to cut Life free from the crystallized effects of their erroneous concepts? To the alchemist the value of prayer is manifold. In addition to the aforesaid benefits, it provides an impetus to enhance his values and further the goal of divine Truth while the mental mold is in the process of coming into physical manifestation.

The call of beloved Jesus at the hour of his greatest testing, "Nevertheless, not my will, but Thine be done!"[1] teaches a more advanced law of Alchemy. When spoken by the alchemist at the moment of the sealing of the matrix, this call ensures that the guiding forces of power, wisdom, and love will amend the precipitated pattern where necessary in order that the more perfect designs of the Creator may come forth in the world of form. This places the whole process of precipitation within the forcefield of eternal perceptions and provides man, as a co-creator with God, with the added benefit of the assistance of the Almighty as he forms and develops his own idea-pattern of destiny in accordance with cosmic purpose.

In my most recent offering, I hinted at the possibility of other minds interfering with the process of precipitation. And while I wish no one to become fearful of this eventuality, I do want each one to be alert to protect himself by guarded silence. Guarded action and guarded meditation are additional guarantees that the freedom to create which God intends all to have will be the lot of everyone. Your visualization of a blue light around yourself, your matrix, and its manifestation will serve to focalize the desired protection.

When Christ Jesus made the statement "Think not that I am come to send peace on earth: I came not to send peace, but a sword," it caused consternation to many who followed him as the Prince of Peace and it has continued to do so to the present hour. Beloved ones, that declaration, together with that which follows—"I am come to set a man at variance against his father and the daughter against her mother and the daughter-in-law against her mother-in-law, and a man's foes shall be they of his own household"[2] —have in common the purpose of conveying a message of protection to each lifestream.

The Savior proclaimed to all mankind the need to protect the very God-design which belongs to them. Therefore, if some should presume to tell others how to live, they would be setting at variance family and friends; and if a man choose consciously to seek, find, and follow his own God-design, although that very pattern may not please father, mother, friends, or society, that man should accept it albeit it set him at variance with those who yet hold the world's concepts of fulfillment.

In following Bethlehem's Star—the inner lodestone of the Christ—one shares Gethsemane, calvary, resurrection's morn, and ascension's hill. Thus no one can have true peace until the sword of divine discrimination enables him to discern Reality for himself and then to protect the inherent gifts and graces God has sealed within him in order to make of each lifestream a glorious facet in the master plan of the creation.

I do not allow that an excuse for human stubbornness should arise from my preceding statement. Surely it should be realized that many well-meaning parents and friends do give sound advice, that many religious and educational leaders do likewise, and that much can be learned from listening to the wisdom of the learned and the well informed. I am, however, interested in each individual's mastering for himself the process of self-discrimination whereby he develops the qualities of leadership and the ability to weigh the advices of others, obediently looking to the God above to penetrate the density of human reason with the Light of His benevolence—which, I repeat, is the dawn and the substance of pure reason itself. Greater logic hath no man than the incomparable wisdom of the Logos!

There is here, nonetheless, a point of danger, a thin-ice state of consciousness where foolish aloofness is sensitized within the student; and in this state he declares, "I need only God, and He alone must tell me all I would know." Well, dear ones, when the King bids the son to a feast, he employs servants to place the goods of his table before the son, who must then arise and partake of it for himself. So let all learn to recognize the true worth in others and in all things, but be not misled by the blindness of others.

Now I come to a place where I am anxious to convey to you a great mystery in a manner whereby the very correctness of your apprehension will enable you to reap permanent benefits in your mind and affairs. It is this: the alchemist's understanding of consciousness as the supreme ingredient.

Beloved ones, with God all things are possible![3] If you possess His Consciousness, then it is now so for each of you—all things are, in fact, immediately possible to you in manifestation. If this is not your instantaneous experience, then you need more of His Consciousness! "So far, so good," you say; "but how do I go about acquiring that nebulous commodity called consciousness?"

Beloved ones, what and where is your consciousness? The minute specks of physical matter or energy, atomic in nature, are composed of particles of Light held within orbital paths, prescribed and imbued with intelligent action. This spiritual magnetism, infused with creative intelligence, power, and love, is a flux whose density permeates the entire sphere and realm of each atom, extending outward into molecular and cellular composition and thence through the elemental phases of nature, manifesting unto planetary scale; and when correctly understood, these particles shall be known to be whirling in infinitely fantastic orbital paths through solar, galactic, and universal densities.

Relative size has enabled mankind to feel that his consciousness is body-confined or cell-confined, as the case may be. This concept of the ghost chained within the human machine is a total mistake. Although the flow of interacting forces may become more complex, still the concept of an expanding consciousness, simultaneous with an expanding universe, must be reckoned with if man will correctly master his affairs.

Man is no more confined to his body than he is to an atom of substance within it or within his brain. Neither are the atoms of physical matter composing that body confined to it and limited in expression by that body or matter-mind density. The power of reaching outward and becoming a part altogether conscious of a whole in a marvelously spiritual manner is the gift of God to all. No one loses any part of that which is already his own by so doing, and no one takes anything away from anyone else through this sharing of the glories of God.

The real meaning of the passage of Scripture in which John the Revelator referred to the little book [4] which would be sweet in the mouth and bitter in the belly relates to his digestion of the idea of himself as containing the universe and the universe containing him. The Book of Life spoken of in Revelation [5] is the lexicon of God, and the lexicon of God embraces the entire Cosmos. Inasmuch as it spans all of the creation, let none take away another's portion or privilege to enjoy all of its cosmic truth; nor let anyone deprive himself of this, life's greatest privilege. To do so is to take away either one's own or another's portion; and surely then God, as Law, shall confine the one so doing to the same sphere of limitation to which he has confined another.

Let all in being their brother's keeper esteem the highest and best possibilities for everyone. Therefore, expand and contract the consciousness to sense not only the necessary internal realm of being, but also the externally expanding universe, and you shall find your consciousness leaping into the arms of the Eternal Alchemist Himself.

Now it is not my intention to leave the many subjects included in this course without a spiritual and physical synopsis and an appendage of daily usefulness. Therefore, the next lesson shall include the golden cord, which should perhaps be spelled *chord;* for it is intended to create a final harmonizing key in consciousness that will make this course of permanent and inestimable value to all.

I am hopefully including such instruction as shall serve to frame the whole in a setting rare and lovely. But the whole herein referred to is your whole life! Master your consciousness by properly directing its attention, and possess thereby the key to God's precious storehouse of eternal substance.

Fondly, I AM

Saint Germain

✠

IX

The Crucible of Being

Breathes there the man, with soul so dead,
Who never to himself hath said,
This is my own, my native universe!

Part I

If I could cite one area of application which the students need to work on more than any other, it is that of the expansion of the universal consciousness within the forcefield of the individual. The greatest need of mankind today—and I say this unequivocally—is the development and the nurturing of the sense of the universal as belonging completely to the individual. From thence is drawn the foregone conclusion that the individual must also be sensed as belonging to that universal Cosmos so conceived.

As the student of Alchemy approaches the temple of Being, of Life, of Oneness, he must, if he would correctly apprehend the meaning of existence and derive happiness therefrom, see himself as a diamond of Light's perfection set in a mounting of perpetual elegance. Acknowledging his origin in those permanent realities which the interpretive mind and heart of Being are able to apprehend and hold in the proper focus of prospective progress, man shall once again renew his intelligently guided drift toward sublime Reality.

There is no greater deterrent to progress than the isolationism that evolves out of the sense of separation from Life wherein the smallness of the ego, pitted against indeterminate odds, lurks in the shadows of uncertainty. The unforeseeable events of the future, by reason of their opacity, project little comfort into the longing heart which awaits some word from the creative Mind of God, some foreknowledge of the depth of that love which God feels for each part of the vast whole of the Cosmos in all of its immensity and greatness.

From the least to the greatest minds of earth, all need the benefit of lasting attunement with the universal Consciousness of God. Mankind, through various religious concepts, have imagined God to be a "creature-creator" simply because they themselves are "creator-creatures." Using the tremendous outgoing energy of Being, men have diligently imagined and imaged forth the nature of God, while only the few have apprehended the truth that God is consciousness, and as consciousness He is life, intelligence, will, and love manifest in a rich variety of dimensions and attributes.

Now I tell you, God is a benign Impersonal Personality, a Personal Impersonality, a Personal Personality, and an Impersonal Impersonality comprising the manifold Consciousness of Being. He gives and gives of

His creative Self to the creatures He has made in the hope that they will apprehend His purposes and emulate His Consciousness to the fullness with which He has endowed them.

As they mature and grow throughout life, people imitate one another, consciously and unconsciously mimicking the personalities that touch their lives. They dwell in such a sense of unreality that they persist in identifying themselves as vile sinners. They accept not only the accusations of the "accuser of our brethren" whose machinations are exposed in the twelfth chapter of the Book of Revelation, but also the burden of mounting waves of mass condemnation which, like a raging sea, threaten to drown the Real Image of the Higher Self in an ocean of emotion.

The purpose of thought and feeling is to form the mold of fruitful and progressive experience which in turn endows mankind with the highest aspects of his Divine Self. You see, blessed alchemists, your thoughts and feelings are the collimation lines that adjust and align your energies, focusing them through the lens of consciousness according to your free will for either constructive or destructive designs in the world of form. Mankind, in the mainstream of their influence, have misused the energies of their thoughts and feelings; and, unaware of the consequences of their mental and emotional inconsistencies, irregularities, and incongruities, they have molded Light's energies descending into their world into asymmetrical forms which, by reason of their nature, could never produce happiness for themselves or any other part of Life.

The idea of a temperamental, vengeful, or unjust God is abhorrent from the outset. The concept of an arbitrary

Deity who would show favoritism is likewise distressing. Hence, according to his awareness of the Deity, man himself becomes the arbiter of his destiny, and, according to his uses of energy, the harbinger of truth or error in his life.

The stratification of human consciousness from the aboriginal types unto the erudite twentieth-century man, skilled in philosophy, science, religion, and the higher mechanics of living, persists in its full range to the present day in various parts of the world. Honest individuals will even recognize in themselves these progressive steps of consciousness which, if progress is being made, are constantly in a state of flux.

Now it is true that it may be more comfortable, at least temporarily, for mankind to vegetate neath the sun and the moon in an isolated reverie, remote from the challenges of life, without benefit of the sometimes violent but always disturbing alchemical heat which, as Christic fires, acts to purge mankind of his dross. But I am certain that the soul which desires to climb the hill of attainment to reach the summit peaks will neither find fault with nor reject the necessary chain of experiences that are intended to broaden the mind, sharpen the intellect, exalt the spirit, and test the mettle of a man.

While on the subject of the gradations of consciousness, remember that each level represents a phase of the alchemy of transition from the human to the divine. A just sense of the equal opportunity of all to apprentice themselves to the Master Alchemist is a prerequisite to personal freedom. To recognize the potential of a mobile and malleable consciousness is to recognize the soaring of the spirit. To be willing to accept personal responsibility for changing unwanted conditions within the domain of the self is to accept the responsibility of being a son of God. Those who cater to their egos and allow the energy patterns (i.e., vibrations) of personal jealousy to block the doorway to self-mastery as they court the attainment of another lifestream will be hindered in their progress on the Path until they have transmuted this propensity.

Jealousy is in fact rooted in the doubt and the fear that Almighty God Himself is unable to bestow upon each one every good and necessary talent contributing to the fulfillment of his divine plan. Inasmuch as jealousy and competition between individual expressions of God are among the basic causes of all unhappiness upon earth, I would definitely underscore the students' need to put them to the Flame. The threats to the alchemist's self-mastery posed by jealousy manifest in many subtle modes—so much so that many honest-hearted people are unaware of the fact that such tainted vibrations do from time to time play upon their feelings.

Application made in prayer and supplication or as invocations and affirmations (called decrees) made in the name of God for the freeing of oneself from all conditions of struggle and strife will bear the fruit of an active yet peaceful progress. You see, false identification with family and friends, the acceptance of limitations through heredity and environment, attachment to persons and places, to one's race, religion, nationality or ethnic group must also be submitted to the flames of the Refiner's fire for transmutation. Personal attitudes must be adjusted to impersonal laws, and thought and feeling patterns must be molded after more noble designs if the individual is to make true spiritual progress. I do not say that individuals should not be loyal to those whom they love and in whom they believe; but I do declare that man's first loyalty should be to his True Self, his own God Identity, and to his Christed Being, and then to those of like mind. Above all, the purposes and uses of Life must be rightly understood and practiced.

To awaken each day to another round of pursuing vain pleasures and the questionable hope of mortal expectation—herein lies a state of flaccid misery in which the soul is scarcely exercised. When the purposes of Heaven are truly understood, man will welcome the dawn and receive each new day with joy. In the fullness of Life man can hardly fear death. As I wrote in my *Essay of Death* (under the name of Francis Bacon), "It is as natural to die as to be born, and to a little infant perhaps the one is as painful as the other!" Thus we now stand at a point in our alchemical studies where we must understand the meaning of the mortification of the body of untransmuted substance.

Through the centuries men have taken great pride in the body: they have glorified it and deified it. Artists have painted it; sculptors have created beautiful statues exhibiting it; and in the end it has fallen into dust and decay. All the while this process of decay has been going on, the spirit of man has supposedly been creating houses of perfection eternal in the heavens.[1] And this is true in part, for every good deed which man does while in the body is recorded to his credit in the great concentric rings of Light and electronic substance which comprise his Causal Body—the body of First Cause which is the dwelling place of the Presence of the Most High God. As each individual man who is a manifestation of God has a Causal Body, so each individual has an "I AM" Presence pulsating as the Sacred Fire in the center of that Body. And in the auric forcefield surrounding that Presence are the markings of his achievements for Good upon his planetary home.

One law, then, would I instill in the hearts of the students of Alchemy: God is absolutely just; the universe is absolutely just. All injustice arises either in man's misinterpretation and misunderstanding of the flow of events or in man's mishandling of justice. Those who have not apprehended life correctly, those who remain ignorant of the laws of divine as well as human justice, cannot be relied upon to preserve the flame of justice.

As I have stated before, every student must be willing to throw off the shackles of the false teachers and their false teachings. Every student must determine to break the chains of error even while he rejects the image of the world as a place where integrity is lacking and the suggestion that individuals are here to take advantage of one another. As the well-known and often-quoted entrepreneur P. T. Barnum said, "A sucker is born every minute." Of course people do not like to think that they are being taken advantage of. Therefore, they often try to outdo the other fellow before he outdoes them; this attitude is responsible for a most unhealthy climate in both commerce and society.

While it is true that the responsibility rests with the world's leaders in every field to set an example of integrity, nothing should prevent the world's followers from manifesting that integrity which their leaders ought to manifest or from exalting virtue as an example before them. There is much in the world's thought about itself that is accurate, but its inaccuracies have come to be accepted by individuals without question. Such tacit acceptance makes for both a weak civilization and a weak individuality.

Therefore, in strengthening the bonds of freedom throughout the world, a new man must emerge from the social milieu: a New Atlantean must step forth clothed with the righteousness of the Sun! A golden man for the Golden Age! This is the Master Alchemist! If this spiritual man—clothed with the power of the Sun, clothed with the power of spiritual Alchemy, clothed with the virtue that he already possesses but of which he is far too often unaware—is to stand forth today, it must be because he has offered the "body" of his corrupt substances to be thrown into the crucible of the alchemical furnace!

The early Christian mystics and writers referred to this experience when they said that a man ought to die with Christ if he expected to live with Him.[2] This death of the old man with his deeds[3] is confined to the crucible of the spiritual-alchemical experience; thus it is possible for all unwanted conditions in a man's life to be changed, that he may pass through a glorious transmutative epic culminating in the putting-on of the new man. Free at last of the dross of the human experience, man stands forth in all of the shining glory of the divine experience that is the wholeness of the resurrection.

The agonies of Gethsemane may be compared to the spiritual preparation that the individual alchemist must make before knowingly and consciously committing himself to the crucible of life in order that he may emerge in the true glory of his being. This is dying with Christ in the certain hope that he will live again.

Beloved ones, bear in mind that those who do not do so willingly and knowingly will still pass through the change called death, even if they persist in following the ways that lead to destruction. But this change, without the prior putting-off of the old man, will not lead to the indestructible Christhood that God intends every son to manifest. It is a supreme demonstration of faith when a living soul, forsaking even self-love, offers himself as a living sacrifice in order that Christ-victory be glorified through him. Such is a career son of God!

In closing Part I, I advocate that the seeker make any sacrifice necessary to the seeking-out of the golden possibilities that gleam through the mists of time and space as spiritual reality—the hope of every man upon earth!

Part II

Beloved ones, just as heaven is not lost by a single thought or deed of a lifestream, so heaven is not gained by a single thought or deed. Nevertheless, your life can become a daily round of victories whereby each step taken aright propels you into an expanding awareness of the beauty and glory of the newness of life. This is the resurrection from dead works of carnality into the living exaltation of the Christ Consciousness of spirituality, vesting each one so dedicated with the mission of Jesus the Christ—one of the greatest alchemists of all time.

Speaking of resurrection, I am reminded of the words "In the beauty of the lilies Christ was born across the sea,/ With a glory in His bosom that transfigures you and me:/ As He died to make men holy, let us live to make men free,/ While God is marching on."[4]

The newly resurrected man—in whom Christ is born, in whom there is a transfiguring glory—is resurrected by the power of change, by the science of divine Alchemy. In him the dawn of each new day takes on a spiritual significance never before experienced. He holds each day as a chalice of opportunity to live free and to make all men free. Then all of Nature, in sweet communion with the yearning of his lifestream to fan the fires of freedom, extends immortal hands of felicity. The trees, the flowers, the rocks, the earth—all of the variegated expressions of nature—bow to that man who has made himself the instrument of freedom and extend to him the care and consideration of the Master Gardener Himself. The Father who created the paradise of God referred to in Genesis is now perceived to be in fact the Creator of all loveliness. The sylphs of the air, the undines of the sea, the fiery salamanders of the flame, and the gnomes of the earth are recognized as elemental spirits created to assist that One Father in bringing forth a kingdom of supreme loveliness and beauty.

It is recognized by the perceptive alchemist that the carnal nature of man has been outpictured in part by the nature kingdom; for the elementals, from the smallest to the greatest, are great mimics of the human scene. As they have taken on human concepts of duality, thorns and thistles, pain and parting have been brought forth upon the screen of Life. Yet with all of the despoiling of the virgin beauty of the earth by mankind's discord and inharmony, much that is lovely has remained, showing that the power of God is greater than the power of the deification of evil.

Through friendship with the servants of God and man in nature, the compassionate alchemist learns to utilize the great spiritual flow of elemental life and finds in the presence of the Holy Spirit a cooperation with nature which formerly he did not even dream existed. Looking upon the blessed earth with the grandeur of its rolling plains, its fertile valleys, and its mountain ranges, gazing upon the crystalline mirrors of its lakes and flowing streams interlacing the terrain and conveying the water element in channels of varying depth, mankind become filled with reverent wonder.

The planetary veins and arteries conveying the tireless energy of the Eternal One from place to place upon the spinning globe of the world, the blue dome of the sky with the golden sun disk to warm and revivify mankind, the silent night with the crystal moon and diadems of stars like unto the Pleiades—all of these are flooded with a sense of unity which pervades all things. Nowhere is unity felt with greater meaning than in the depths of the heart of the individual who is in complete attunement with God and his own I AM Presence, the individualized identity of the perfection of the Creator Himself.

That body of historical error composed of myriad carnal events and human misqualifications is changed now by the alchemical fires of spiritual regeneration, and in its place the wholeness of the Real Being of man stands forth. He is no longer a part: he is the all of creation! These valleys and hills, these diadems of stars and far reaches of space are a part of himself. He is all of them and in them all! With this supernal sense of ever-present wonder, man is able, as an integral manifestation of God, to perform the miracles of the Great Alchemist and make his world the wondrous glory of the resurrection! Old senses are passed away; all things are become new.[5]

With that I wish to give the students a coup d'oeil into advancements which shall be forthcoming in the world of science. I am interested in offering a preview of man's greater control of the elements in this *Studies in Alchemy,* because some of our would-be alchemists can be instrumental in the production of these new techniques or in calling them forth from the Universal.

Let us consider for a moment the development of the mind-switch. At present, lights, elevators, doors, and many devices are activated by switches or electronically; and engineers are at work upon a typewriter which will type phonetically sentences spoken directly into it. The mind-switch is even more revolutionary, for it will enable men to direct mechanical apparatus and electrical functions through brain waves by the mastery of the energy currents flowing through the mind. Of course many amusing situations could be construed in which two individuals might transmit divergent impulses simultaneously. This should pose no problem; for they would but cancel each other out or the stronger would overcome the weaker of the transmitted thought waves.

Another development of the coming age will be a camera so sensitized that it will make possible the photographing of the human aura. This will enable physicians to discover the fundamental causes of many physical diseases as well as the solution to psychiatric problems related to the emotions and subconscious records of past experiences, even in previous lives unknown to the patients themselves. The wave patterns caused by criminal tendencies and crimes recorded in the etheric body will also be "photographed," or recorded by sensitive instruments in graphic form similar to the process now used to record brain waves and impulses of the nervous system. Evidence of guilt or innocence will thereby be afforded those administrators of justice who formerly relied on incomplete knowledge of events in the penalizing of delinquent individuals.

With the advent of greater understanding of magnetism, it will be possible to so amplify the power of magnetism as to suspend furniture in midair without any form of visible support. A new optical development is forthcoming which will increase mankind's exploration of the submicroscopic and atomic worlds. In this field the magnification of images with great clarity will become possible by methods not previously encountered. With this advancement certain methods of transmutation will be made known to the chemists of the world whereby the synthesis of new elements will be achieved as simply as a child plays with blocks.

A new form of aeronavigation and transportation will be made possible by utilizing an electronic ray played upon the metal of which the airship itself is composed, negating the gravitational influences upon it and giving it a quality of lightness similar to helium. This will enable it to rise in complete resistance to the power of gravity. The ship can then be directed by atomic jets in such a manner that a safer form of locomotion will be made available to all. A breakthrough in color television enabling increased clarity in the ranges of color tones and values should come forth before too long.

Through the means of orbiting satellites such as those that are currently circling the earth, a new method of studying the weather and of mapping it will cause mankind to realize the need for a central control station for the weather in order to direct its conditions over most of the landed areas of the world. I feel, however, that this could be the subject of much controversy and may eventually be dropped until the time when greater unity and amicability exist between various interest groups and among the family of nations.

The work begun many years ago by Luther Burbank—who acted under the direction of the Hierarchy in his experiments with nature and the grafting of plants—

will be brought to a new degree of perfection as certain influences within the hearts of the seeds themselves are revealed through advanced studies in cytology. Within the heart of the desert cactus is locked a secret whereby the arid areas of the world can indeed be made to blossom as the rose[6] and produce all manner of fruits and vegetables with far less moisture than is presently required. Water shortages may thus be alleviated.

The present surge in world population, which seems to have caused many demographers to review and revise the doctrines of Malthus with the aim of extinguishing or limiting human life in complete contradiction to God's laws, will prove of less concern to future societies as they become aware of marvelous methods of increasing agricultural production, of harvesting the wealth of the sea, and of the unlimited use of atomic energy in advanced city planning as well as in interplanetary colonization.

There is a purpose in the plans of God which far transcends the understanding of the human intellect and the memory of history upon earth. The wonders that are to come will soon be dwarfed by still greater wonders, and therefore all Life should live in a state of constant expectancy. It is the joy of the Mind of God to give richly of His blessing. But above all, may I counsel you now, students of the Light and all mankind: Obtain first from God the Father the wisdom to live peaceably, to deal gently and courteously with one another, to promote the education of mankind the world around, and especially by honest efforts to prevent the increase in number of those indigent individuals who are prone to commit crimes against society.

The value of training the young in a proper manner and encouraging them to live lives of useful service and good character cannot be overestimated. Political scandals within the nations of the world and the harshness of police-state methods (as enforced in communist-dominated countries) must be overridden by the sword of the Prince of Peace. The Prince of Peace is imaged in the compassionate Christ going forth to teach all nations that the way of God is good, that His wonders are intended to be used and possessed by all and exclusively by none. A higher way of life than vain competition must be pursued. Men must become God-spurred and less motivated by status seeking. Teach this truth! The sharing of the grace of Heaven is a message of eternal watchfulness from the Great White Brotherhood to all upon earth.

Abundance and peace go hand in hand, and this state of felicity is the will of God. Let this planet, by the power of spiritual and natural alchemy, arise to build new homes, new churches, new schools, a new civilization, new concepts, new virtue, new greatness—all in the bonds of eternal confidence which blazes forth from the very Heart of God and is anchored within your own physical heart as the expanding flame spark of the Immortal Alchemist Himself!

Part III

The feeling of aloneness should be transmuted and superseded by the certainty of all-oneness. Man came forth from God as good, and he shall return to that goodness by becoming like it through the dignity of freedom and choice. The power, love, and wisdom of God are never tyrannical, but gently bestow upon each individual creature of the creation the blessedness of opportunity to know God without limit. Forgiveness, mercy, justice, peace, achievement, and progress toward ultimate supremacy are the gifts which Life holds for all.

Through the process of descent into matter and form, man, as a part of God destined to become ultimately victorious, is made the conscious master of all he surveys, so long as he is not forgetful of his Source. By identifying with the gross, man becomes almost at once entangled in a web of human creation whose snarls, like the thread of Ariadne weaving through the labyrinthian cave of subterranean matter, bring him face to face with the Minotaur who dwells in the lower octaves of consciousness waiting to devour the Christ.

Escape is freedom. That which descends and is committed to form and density must, in obtaining its freedom, ascend back to that Source from whence it came. To do this prematurely is in error; and therefore the Father, or I AM Presence, knows of each lifestream the day and hour when he is truly ready! Until the fullness of outer circumstance is transcended and transmuted in a manner whereby the lifestream has fulfilled his original purposes for entering the orbit of earth, he should continue his training and preparation in accordance with the universal plan.

Surely thoughtful individuals will quickly recognize that marrying and the giving in marriage, procreation and the perpetuation of present modes of civilization are not of themselves the ultimate purposes of Life. All the world as a stage is not the cosmic coliseum; and ere the curtain is drawn on the final act, the drama of man's existence shall be played out in many corners of the universe undreamed of by either early or modern man. Men's dreams of heaven are but fond glimpses into the imagery of Elysium graciously afforded mankind as encouragement until the time when they are able to expand their own spiritual vision and behold reality in the wonders of the Father in His many cosmic mansions.

The supreme purpose of God for every lifestream upon earth is the selfsame victory which beloved Jesus manifested from the hill of Bethany. The accent of Christendom upon the agony of Gethsemane, the crucifixion, and the vigil in the tomb of Joseph of Arimathea has often eclipsed the great significance for every man, woman, and child of the glories of the resurrection and mysteries of the ascension.

Misunderstanding of the law of cause and effect and failure to apprehend the at-one-ment of the Universal Christ originated in the human concepts that were introduced in the parable of Eden and continue to the present day, perpetuated by the hoary mists of time and dogma. Unfortunately, the vicarious atonement has been ignorantly accepted and is widely used as an excuse for wrongdoings and their continuation. Thus, surrounded by an aura of godly but needless fear, men have persisted in passing on fallacies from generation to generation in the name of God and Holy Writ.

The registering of discord and wrongdoing upon man's four lower bodies (i.e., the physical, mental, memory, and emotional bodies) is effected by scientific law, cosmically ordained and itself the very instrument of creation. As creators, men have sown the wind and reaped a karmic whirlwind.[7] The victory of the Universal Christ, which beloved Jesus demonstrated, was intended to show to man the way that would conduct him safely back to God's Image. That way was revealed as the Christ, or Divine Light, within every man that cometh into the world.[8] It is this wondrous Light, then, which is the Light and Life of the world—of every man's individual world. Only by walking in the Light as He, the Universal Christ, is in the Light can men return to the Father's house.

The forgiveness of sins is a merciful instrument of the Great Law whereby retribution, or the penalty for wrongdoing, is held in abeyance in order that a lifestream may have the freedom to "go and sin no more"[9] and then be given the opportunity for greater spiritual progress. However, forgiveness does not absolve the soul of the requirement to balance the energies misused by the alchemical fires of transmutation. The balancing of wrongs done to every part of Life, including the self, must be accomplished in full with cosmic precision; hence every jot and tittle of the Law must be fulfilled[10] either here or hereafter. This process need not be a fearful looking-for of judgment,[11] but it should preferably be a happy expectation of opportunity for service to Life and the freeing of Life's imprisoned splendor. For by ministering unto Life individually and universally and by calling forth the alchemical fires on the altar of Being, the individual can undo all of the inharmonies which he has thoughtlessly cast upon its beauteous presence. Truly, those who have been forgiven much can love much;[12] for they perceive the need to be everlastingly grateful for the goodness and mercy of God which endure forever![13]

One of the major causes of recalcitrance, arrogance, willful wrongdoing, disobedience, rebellion, and stubbornness is the vain hope of individual attainment without individual effort or of personal salvation without personal sacrifice. Mankind do not relish the idea of painstakingly withdrawing every thread and snarl they have placed in the garment of life or of attaining Heaven by honest application. Yet they must one day face this truth of themselves; therefore, the present, when truth and justice of opportunity are at hand, is the right and accepted time. "Behold, now is the accepted time; behold, now is the day of salvation."[14]

The desire to find a scapegoat for one's sins in a world teacher or savior is not in keeping with the cosmic principles undergirding the law of the atonement. A Master of great Light such as Jesus the Christ or Gautama Buddha may hold the balance for millions of souls who are not able to carry the weight of their own sinful sense. This holding action is a staying of the Law whereby, through mercy and through the personal sacrifice of one who keeps the Flame for all, mankind might find their way back to God and then, in the power of the rebirth and in the presence of the Holy Spirit, return to take up the unfinished business of balancing their debts to Life. Christ is the savior of the world because by His immaculate heart He postpones the day of judgment, affording humanity additional opportunity in time and space to fulfill the requirements of immortality.

I cannot, in the holy name of freedom, resist speaking out on these matters; for many have suffered in the astral world after the change called death, and when they came before the Lords of Karma to give an accounting for their lives, they were found wanting. Unfortunately, this may have been only because while on earth they accepted false religious doctrine and, in their misguided state, failed to do well in the time allotted to them. Then came to pass the words God spake to Adam "Sin lieth at the door"[15]—that is to say, the record of the misuse of God's energy is at hand: render an accounting.

In God's scheme of world order, the propitiation for sin is permanent and effective; for the violet fire will transmute every unwanted condition and balance all by Light. This Light is the Universal Christ. The precious violet flame, an aspect of the Comforter's [16] Consciousness, is the friend of every alchemist. It is both the cup and the elixir of Life that cannot fail to produce perfection everywhere when it is called into action. After the violet flame has performed its perfect work, then let all rest in their labors that God may move upon the waters (waves of Light) of the creation to produce and sustain the righteousness of His eternal Law.

The climax or initiation of the ascension can and will come to all, even to little children, when they are ready for it—when at least 51 percent of their karma has been balanced (this means that 51 percent of all the energy ever given to their use has been transmuted and put to constructive purpose) and their hearts are just toward God and man, aspiring to rise into the never-failing Light of God's eternally ascending Presence.

When this gift is given to anyone by his own I AM Presence and the Karmic Board, the appearance of age drops from him as swiftly as a smile can raise the lips, and the magnetism and energy of that one becomes the unlimited power of God surging through his being. The dross of the physical, the weariness of the emotional body, tired of hatred and its monstrous creations, the ceaseless rote of the mental body—all drop away and are replaced in perfect ease by their divine counterparts. The feelings become charged by the love of God and the angels; the mind is the Diamond Shining Mind of God—omnipresent, omniscient, omnipotent. The total being is inspired and aspiring!

Thus that which once hopefully descended now ascends back into the Light from whence it came. One with

77

the company of angels and the nature and friendship of the Ascended Masters and in fellowship with the august fraternity of the Great White Brotherhood, each such one, by the divine merit within, attains the fullness of all that God would ever bestow upon each son without respect of any man's person, but in joyful acknowledgment of man's victory: Thou art My beloved son, this day have I begotten thee![17]

Epilogue

Religion and spirituality are no shame. These are the implements of the eternally creative arts. These are the friends of the alchemist who would change every base element of human nature and all life into the gold of Christed accomplishment. In this teaching are keys to the highest portal. They must be fitted in the lock to gain entrance to the highest initiation. I AM the door to the progressive unfoldment of ever-ascending planes of consciousness—all within your lovely God Presence I AM.

Blessed ones, you are not limited in Alchemy merely to the drawing-forth from the universal Light of three-dimensional objects. Alchemy can be mastered in order to illumine the mind, to heal any unwanted condition, and to spiritually exalt man's total nature from its base state to the golden standard where the Golden Rule is law. With you—as with God—all things are possible.[18] There is no other or higher way. For example, the brilliance of present Soviet science cannot win the universe for the blessed children of Mother Russia. Only God can bring eternal satisfaction to the whole earth. Let the ungodly tremble, for they shall be cut down as grass;[19] but the righteous shall shine as the sons of the Great Alchemist, Almighty God!

Further studies in Alchemy are available to all who would progressively advance in this science of self-dominion. Some of this material I am releasing in the lessons of the Keepers of the Flame Fraternity, some in the weekly *Pearls of Wisdom* written by the Masters of our Brotherhood, and some I shall bring to you individually in answer to your heart's calls. But call you must if this cause which is just shall be fulfilled in you!

"Call unto Me and I will answer thee," [20] declares the Most High God. The Father shall reward you openly for each prayerful call you make in secret. [21] Within the inner recesses of your heart, unknown by any man, you may ever silently call. There in your heart is the crucible of the eternal essence, the White Stone, the elixir and full potency of Life.

Alchemists of the Sacred Fire, here is the sacred cosmic formula: Theos = God; Rule = Law; You = Being; *Theos + Rule + You = God's Law active as Principle within your Being (TRY).*

I AM in constant attunement with your true Being,

Pax vobiscum

Sanctus Germanus

✠

79

Biographical Sketch

Holding the title of God of Freedom to this system of worlds, Saint Germain has stood for centuries as the defender of individual and world freedom.

On Atlantis he served in the Order of Lord Zadkiel as High Priest in the Temple of Purification. Midst marble halls glistening white, surrounded by ancient pines whose branches blended with the winds of the Holy Spirit, his invocations sustained a pillar of fire, a veritable fountain of violet singing flame that magnetized the great and the small who came from near and far to be set free from every binding condition of body, soul, and mind. Here gathered nature spirits and angel devas in praise of one whose love was ever the source of regenerative hope and joyous freedom to outpicture in the nature kingdom the geometric forms of truth and freedom, mercy and justice.

Prior to the sinking of Atlantis, while Noah was yet building his ark and warning the people of the great Flood to come, Saint Germain, accompanied by a few faithful priests, transported the flame of freedom from the Temple of Purification to a place of safety in the Carpathian foothills in Transylvania. Here they carried on the sacred ritual of expanding the fires of freedom even while mankind's karma was being exacted by divine decree. In succeeding embodiments, under the guidance of his master and teacher, the Great Divine Director, Saint Germain and his followers rediscovered the flame and continued to guard the shrine. Later the Great Divine Director, assisted by his disciple, established a retreat at the site of the flame and founded the House of Rakoczy.

This same flame, brilliant in its transmutative radiance like the color of cattleya orchids, has been focused in the etheric retreat of Archangel Zadkiel and Holy Amethyst above the island of Cuba since the early days of Atlantis. In the fifteenth century Destiny smiled again upon the son of freedom: an arc from the flame in the retreat leaped into the heart of the young man now embodied in the little town of Genoa as the relatively unknown sailor, Christopher Columbus (1451-1506). Fate had sent out a line and, despite all obstacles, the captain of the *Santa Maria* was drawn to the shores of a New World.

As Christopher (meaning Light-bearer) Columbus, Saint Germain charted a path of freedom that millions were destined to follow. No wonder! For at that very retreat he had practiced the sacred science of Alchemy over a period of centuries both between and during his many embodiments, sponsored by the Archangel and Archaeia of the Seventh Ray. For Christopher Columbus the New World was home port; and, appropriately, angels of the Sacred Fire were there on the island of San Salvador to welcome the three ships on that triumphant October 12th in 1492.

As the prophet Samuel (meaning "his name is God"), Saint Germain heard the Voice of God and responded, "Speak Lord; for thy servant heareth."[1] And it is recorded that "Samuel grew, and the Lord was with him, and did let none of his words fall to the ground. And all Israel from Dan even to Beersheba knew that Samuel was established to be a prophet of the Lord."[2] Samuel—anointer of kings, oracle of the people, confidant of Saul and David—one day would be held affectionately in the hearts of a people sworn to a mighty union as "Uncle Sam."

Having assisted in laying the spiritual foundations of Israel, Saint Germain invoked the Christ Flame for the Christian Dispensation when he was embodied as Joseph, the protector of Jesus and Mary—always close at hand when he was needed, lending his strong arm in defense of Mother and Child.

In the third century this holy brother laid down his life for Amphibalus, another devout Christian, and became the first martyr of England, later canonized as Saint Alban. As Merlin, "the wise old man," he assisted King Arthur (El Morya) in framing the Holy Order of the Knights of the Round Table and in establishing the quest for the Holy Grail,* the cup from which our Lord drank at the Last Supper.

When Saint Germain was embodied as Roger Bacon (1214-1294), he authored *Opus Majus* and other well-known treatises on physics, chemistry, and mathematics. As Francis Bacon (1561-1626), he was the *fils naturel* of Queen Elizabeth and Lord Leicester, the rightful heir to the throne of England. He translated the King James version

---

* The Holy Grail was carried by boat to the British Isles by Mary, the Mother of Jesus, assisted by Joseph of Arimathea and several others who made the pilgrimage with her, establishing focuses at Lourdes and Fatima, which would later be used for her visitations. The cup, traditionally associated with the town of Glastonbury, became the focal point for the spread of Christianity during the period of British colonization.

of the Bible and wrote the *Novum Organum* and the Shakespearean plays, which contain in code many of the sacred mysteries of the Brotherhood, as well as the story of his life. After completing the work he had set out to do in that embodiment, he made his exit in his usual good humor by attending his own funeral in 1626. (The body in the coffin was not that of Francis Bacon.)

On May 1, 1684, Saint Germain accepted his immortal freedom, which he had espoused and won over a period of thousands of years by making, he says without exaggeration, "two million right decisions." Thus Francis Bacon, hero of letters who through his writings has lived in the hearts of millions, is truly immortal. He ascended from the Rakoczy Mansion in Transylvania where he had been practicing spiritual Alchemy since his departure from the world scene in 1626. The Ascended Master Saint Germain entered the Great Silence (Nirvana), where his beloved twin flame Portia, the Goddess of Justice*—whose name he had inscribed in *The Merchant of Venice*—had long been waiting his return.

Not long thereafter, the beloved Sanctus Germanus entered the cosmic service of freedom and was given the dispensation by the Lords of Karma to function in the world of form as an Ascended Being taking on the appearance of a physical body at will. Thus, throughout the courts of eighteenth-century Europe he was known as the Comte de Saint Germain. He appeared, disappeared, and reappeared in and out of royal circles with his outstanding quality of realism in an age that was closing in upon itself by the weight of its own hypocrisy.[3]

Voltaire aptly described him in a letter to Frederick

* Also known as the Goddess of Opportunity, since justice is love's opportunity to right all wrong and balance Life's energies.

II of Prussia as "a man who never dies, and who knows everything."[4] The archives of France contain evidence that English, Dutch, and Prussian statesmen of his time regarded the Count as an authority in many fields. He was hated by some while loved and held in awe by others. Yet Saint Germain's real mission—the carrying of the torch of freedom for the age—has not been understood by historians.

Quite naturally the Master Alchemist spoke French, German, English, Italian, Spanish, Portuguese, and Russian, in addition to classical Greek, Roman, Sanskrit, Chinese, and Arabic. He composed, improvised, accompanied on the piano without music, and played the violin "like an orchestra." His compositions are in the British Museum and the library of the castle of Raudnitz in Bohemia. He painted in oils with colors of gemlike brilliance, which he himself discovered. He maintained an alchemical laboratory, was an adept in precipitating and perfecting gems, transmuting base metals into gold, and discovering herbs and elixirs to prolong life and maintain health. To intimates he displayed powers bordering on the incomprehensible.

Many of his demonstrations of mastery are described in the diaries of Mme. d'Adhemar, who knew him for at least half a century. She records Saint Germain's visits to herself and to the courts of Louis XV and Louis XVI, noting his glowing countenance and appearance of a man in his early forties throughout the period. She mentions a personal conversation with the Count in 1789 in which he appeared "with the same countenance as in 1760, while mine was covered with furrows and marks of decrepitude."[5] In the same conversation he predicted the Revolution of 1789, the fall of the House of Bourbon, and the course of modern French history. More important than these spectacular feats, however, was the use to which the Master put his talents. As one of his friends said, "He was, perhaps, one of the greatest philosophers who ever lived.... his heart was concerned only with the happiness of others."[6]

He was an intimate of Louis XV, who gave him a suite at the Royal Chateau at Chambord. Introducing the science of modern diplomacy, he carried out many secret diplomatic missions for the king to the courts of Europe. Had Saint Germain's counsels been heeded by Louis XVI, they would have prevented the French Revolution and saved the lives of many who were sacrificed at the guillotine. Having failed to prevent the French Revolution, he sought to establish a United States of Europe under Napoleon Bonaparte. But neither the crown, the nobility, nor "le petit caporal" caught the vision of the master plan. As Saint Germain later reflected upon this experience he said:

"Long ago, individuals at the Court of France thought to deceive me. They considered me to be a charlatan, but I fear that I have outlived them and their usefulness; for many of them who dwelled in positions of grandeur in the outer world of form are presently engaged in sweeping the streets of some of these larger cities. Thus, the Law, coming full circle, has exacted from them the very demands that they placed upon those whom they thought to be inferior in their time."[7] In a later dictation he said:

"Having failed in securing the attention of the Court of France and others of the crowned heads of Europe, I turned myself to the perfectionment of mankind at large, and I recognized that there were many who, hungering and thirsting after righteousness, would indeed be filled with the concept of a perfect union which would inspire them to take dominion over the New World and create a union among the sovereign states. Thus the United States was born as a child of my heart and the American Revolution was the means of bringing freedom in all of its glory into manifestation from the East unto the West."[8]

The United States has indeed prospered with the assistance of this Master. Ever behind the scenes to see that liberty should not perish from the earth, he broke the deadlock and inspired the early American patriots to sign the Declaration of Independence. It was he who shouted, "Sign that document!" from the balcony of Independence Hall. He stood by General Washington through the long winter at Valley Forge; and when it came time to dedicate a new nation, conceived in liberty, he assisted in the framing of the Constitution.

In the early 1930s he contacted his "general in the field," the reembodied George Washington, whom he trained as a Messenger for the Hierarchy and who, under the pen name of Godfre Ray King, released the foundation of Saint Germain's instruction for the New Age in *Unveiled Mysteries, The Magic Presence,* and *The "I AM" Discourses.* During this period the Goddess of Justice and other Cosmic Beings came forth from the Great Silence to assist Saint Germain in bringing the teachings of the Sacred Fire to mankind to pave the way for the Golden Age. During the same period the Master undertook the training of the Messengers Mark and Elizabeth Prophet, who were later called by the Chief of the Darjeeling Council, El Morya, to establish The Summit Lighthouse as another open door for the release of Ascended Master instruction to mankind.

Saint Germain maintains a focus in the Golden

Etheric City over the Sahara Desert, where he brought a great civilization to its height seventy thousand years ago. He is also the Hierarch of the etheric retreat over the Rakoczy Mansion in Transylvania and of the Cave of Symbols, his focus in America. His electronic pattern is the Maltese cross; his fragrance, that of violets.

While serving in the world of form as the Comte de Saint Germain, the Master assumed the office of Chohan of the Seventh Ray, which had been held by Kwan Yin, the Goddess of Mercy, for the previous two-thousand-year period. On May 1, 1954, he and his twin flame were crowned the Directors of the two-thousand-year cycle we are now entering—known as the Seventh Dispensation, which comes under the activities of the seventh ray. During this era mankind will be given the opportunity of mastering himself and his environment through the correct knowledge of the laws of true freedom and justice, the science of alchemy, of precipitation and transmutation, and the rituals of invocation to the Sacred Fire that can bring in an age of enlightenment and peace such as the world has never known.

Pursuing his ultimate plan "for the perfectionment of mankind"—which has the approval of the Lords of Karma and the Spiritual Hierarchy in charge of the enlightenment of the age—Saint Germain assisted in the founding of the Keepers of the Flame Fraternity under the auspices of The Summit Lighthouse and accepted the position of Knight Commander of the order. In a letter addressed to the fraternity shortly after its formation Saint Germain said:

"The requirements of the hour are constancy, harmony, and loyalty! For centuries men have tasted of the treasures of heaven, and for an equal time they have debated, delayed and strained at the proper use of those same treasures. The heaven that might have manifested long ago upon earth has been delayed solely by man, and through no fault of the Father, whose kingdom is still in the process of 'coming'! Today the cosmic wheel has turned almost to the point of no return and it is imperative for all mankind that the necessary unity and other divine qualities be forthcoming with expediency.

"In this hour of great testing and decision, I say there is no peril so great as that of impeding or stopping the progress of activities sponsored by the Ascended Masters. As long as there are men and women of faith and goodwill who will lovingly band together with almost fierce loyalty under the Father's aegis and our right hand of fellowship, we will continue to provide the assistance from our level that is so necessary in carrying out upon earth the cosmic-purposed actions that fan the fires of freedom and keep aloft the torch of God-liberty!

"Recently the Darjeeling Council through the beloved Ascended Master El Morya, your friend and mine, made known the formation of a spiritual fraternity to be composed of dedicated men and women who are willing to put their shoulders, minds, and hearts to the wheel of sponsorship in the coordination of the manifold activities under our direction. This voluntary group of 'the faithful' is destined, if they will accept it, to be a part of the selective focus from which shall be drawn the permanent focus of beloved Morya's Diamond Heart (dedicated to the will of God) in the outer world of form. Now I AM honored to acknowledge the first tangible gleams from the hearts of those blessed ones who have accepted with dignity and joy the real privilege of becoming Keepers of the Flame!

"Beloved ones, millions have possessed, but few have retained their possessions. This is true of the Spirit as well as of the flesh. To love God is good, but to love Him with dependable constancy is far better! Yet, the slip between the cup and the lip lies in sheer vacillation; for even the downward way seems paved with so-called good intentions. To change this for the better and then the best is our intention. For we have pledged to continue to supply the wisdom and God-direction if you will make the necessary applications faithfully. Herein lies the saving grace for the earth as well as for man: in conscious unity, faith, constancy, and determination, as much your own as my own!"

In his *Pearl of Wisdom* dated September 17, 1967, Saint Germain made the following statement concerning the Keepers of the Flame Fraternity:

"In this day and age we have entrusted the teachings to no one man, but we have given finite portions of the Infinite, segments of Reality to the planet, as cosmic cipher which the heart, when purified in any man, can readily decipher. In the *Pearls of Wisdom,* the Keepers of the Flame Lessons and other expressions which comprise the teachings of The Summit Lighthouse, we have sought to integrate the wholeness of all genuine uplift movements that have ever existed upon the planet.

"Ours is the intent, as God wills it, if man wills it too and serves with God, to elucidate through the Keepers of the Flame Lessons such standards of elder beauty as have never before been known and experienced upon this planet. The day will come when those souls who are privileged to receive these communications will esteem them as the golden illumined Light of the hand of heaven, reaching into the individual heart and saying, 'Know God, know thyself, know the Law of thy Being.' As never before we hope to open the ancient books—even the books of the

Ancient of Days—to reveal that which has been kept secret since the foundation of the world."

Continuity of purpose is perhaps the most outstanding virtue of Saint Germain. Over a period of hundreds and thousands of years, he has never moved from the central theme of his high calling as a son of God. Ever constant to his mission to free the Christ in all men, ever kindling in them the regenerative hope of freedom, he has carried the torch of liberty on behalf of humanity and stands ready to pass it to those who will "come out from among them" and keep the Flame with him. This is the meaning of keeping the Flame and of being "my brother's keeper."

Saint Germain invites stalwart men and women of the ages to join in the vanguard of freedom; for he says that only when the many join hands with the few who have kept the holy fires burning will freedom become a universal birthright to every man, woman, and child on the planet. To this end do the Keepers of the Flame serve, to this end do they espouse the ancient motto of the Brotherhood: To Know, to Dare, to Do, and to Be Silent.

Notes

Chapter I

1. Matt. 5:45.
2. Matt. 11:12.

Chapter II

1. John 2:1-11.
2. 1 Pet. 4:18.

Chapter III

1. Matt. 5:13.
2. Gen. 19:26.
3. 2 Tim. 2:15.

Chapter IV

1. Heb. 13:2.
2. Heb. 12:1.
3. Heb. 11:6.
4. Amos 5:4.
5. Matt. 19:26.

Chapter V

1. Matt. 11:2-5.
2. Exod. 5:6-19.
3. Luke 22:42.

Chapter VI

1. Mark 8:22-26.
2. Rev. 22:17.
3. Matt. 9:17.

Chapter VII

1. Gen. 1:3.
2. Luke 10:37.
3. John 2:1-11.
4. Matt. 14:19-21.
5. 2 Chron. 7:1-3; 2 Kings 1:10.
6. Matt. 4:3.
7. Matt. 6:33.
8. Heb. 11:1.

Chapter VIII

1. Luke 22:42.
2. Matt. 10:34-36.
3. Matt. 19:26.
4. Rev. 10:9.
5. Rev. 22:18-19.

Chapter IX

1. 2 Cor. 5:1.
2. 1 Cor. 15:31.
3. Eph. 4:22; Col. 3:9.
4. Julia Ward Howe, "Battle Hymn of the Republic," st. 5.
5. 2 Cor. 5:17.
6. Isa. 35:1.
7. Hosea 8:7.
8. John 1:9.
9. John 8:11.
10. Matt. 5:18.

11. Heb. 10:27.
12. Luke 7:47.
13. Pss. 136.
14. 2 Cor. 6:2.
15. Gen. 4:7.
16. John 14:16, 26.
17. Pss. 2:7.
18. Matt. 19:26.
19. Pss. 37:1-2.
20. Jer. 33:3.
21. Matt. 6:6.

Biographical Sketch

1. 1 Sam. 3:9-10.

2. 1 Sam. 3:19-20.

3. See Isabel Cooper-Oakley, **The Comte de St. Germain: The Secret of Kings** (London: Theosophical Publishing House, 1912) Library of Congress Catalog Card Number BF 1598, .S3Cb and bibliography.

4. Ibid., p. 96.

5. Ibid., p. 87.

6. Ibid., p. 1.

7. **Saint Germain's Class of Malta**, 2 vols. (Colorado Springs: The Summit Lighthouse, 1967), 1:8.

8. Ibid., 2:77.

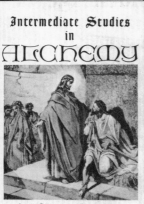

Intermediate Studies in ALCHEMY

by Saint Germain

CAN YOU CREATE A CLOUD?

Those who accept the challenge CAN through instruction given by Saint Germain in INTERMEDIATE STUDIES IN ALCHEMY In handsome paperback edition

"Not what might be, but what will be; because man envisions, invokes, and equates with Universal Law. Alchemy! the wondrous science of change that fulfills the heart's deepest desires, orders man's affairs, and renews the sweet purity of his original communion with the Great Progenitor.

"Now, the identity of the alchemist is to be found in the mandate 'Create!' and in order that he might obey, the fiery energies of creation are dispensed to him each moment. Like crystal beads descending upon a crystal thread, the energies of the creative essence of Life descend into the chalice of consciousness. Neither halting nor delaying in their appointed course, they continue to fall into the repository of man's being. Here they create a buildup for good or for ill as each iota of universal energy passes through the recording nexus and is imprinted with the fiat of creation.

"Now one of the most effective means by which change can be produced—and this which I here make known to you is a deep and wondrous secret held by many of the Eastern and Western adepts—is through what I will call the 'creation of a Cloud.' Saint Paul referred to a 'cloud of witnesses.' I am referring to a Cloud of infinite energy which, somewhat like the ether so popularized by the scientists a century ago, is everywhere present, but nowhere manifest until it is called into action."

These paragraphs from the absorbing cosmic instruction by Saint Germain beckon the souls of men to answer the mandate "Create!" If you desire to explore this thrilling concept, order your copy of INTERMEDIATE STUDIES IN ALCHEMY, a sequel to the popular STUDIES IN ALCHEMY. Here is the key that will open the door to your own immortal destiny!

$2.95 postpaid

FRIENDS OF SAINT GERMAIN: INVEST IN THE YOUTH OF AMERICA. GIVE A SET OF ALCHEMY I AND II TO YOUR LOCAL LIBRARY AND ENCOURAGE CAMPUS BOOKSTORES TO CARRY THE MASTERS' TEACHINGS ON ALCHEMY.

THE SUMMIT LIGHTHOUSE
Box A, Colorado Springs, CO 80901
Box 1227, Santa Barbara, CA 93102

Your Guide to the Golden Age

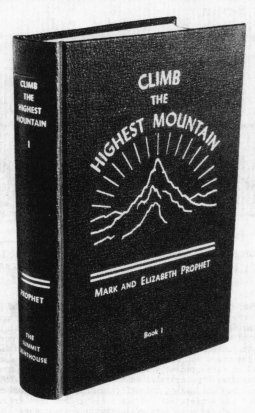

This Is the Book of the Century!

CLIMB THE HIGHEST MOUNTAIN
Book I of THE EVERLASTING GOSPEL
By Mark and Elizabeth Prophet

This magnificent work contains over five hundred pages of instruction in cosmic law, twenty-eight illustrations by the internationally known artist Auriel Bessemer, two color plates, charts and tables, and a comprehensive index. Table of Contents: Chapter 1. **Your Synthetic Image**—An Allegory; The Quest for Reality; The Soul: A Living Potential; The Dethroning of the Synthetic Image; The Enthroning of the Real Image; Chapter 2. **Your Real Image**—The Light Emanation of Eternal Purpose; The Spirit: Birthless, Deathless, Eternal; God the Macrocosm, Man the Microcosm; The Invasion of the Microcosmic Circle; Manifest Immortality: Putting on the New Man; Vestiges of the

**To be a Keeper of the Flame
is a high and noble privilege—
greater before God than any other!**

THE KEEPERS OF THE FLAME FRATERNITY, sponsored by the Knight Commander Saint Germain, is composed of a body of students who have pledged to support the activities of the Ascended Masters in their efforts to reach mankind through The Summit Lighthouse. In return, these students receive instruction on the various aspects of cosmic law, leading to individual self-mastery, Christhood, and preparation for the ascension in the Light. No charge is made for these lessons.

The nominal dues of $3 monthly are given by each member to sponsor, sustain, and expand the activities of The Summit Lighthouse in its worldwide program of bringing the teachings of the Great White Brotherhood to all peoples. Membership also includes the privilege of attending closed classes at the quarterly conferences. The initial fee of $10 includes the first month's dues. Husband and wife or any two members of the same immediate family are admitted for one fee and receive one lesson and two separate cards. Write for free brochure.

THE SUMMIT LIGHTHOUSE
Box A, Colorado Springs, CO 80901
Box 1227, Santa Barbara, CA 93102

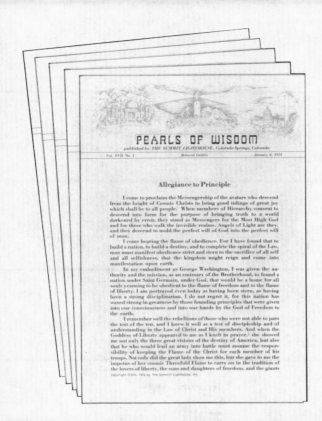

PEARLS OF WISDOM

published by THE SUMMIT LIGHTHOUSE, Colorado Springs, Colorado

Vol. XVII No. 1   Beloved Godfre   January 6, 1974

Allegiance to Principle

I come to proclaim the Messengership of the avatars who descend from the height of Cosmic Christs to bring good tidings of great joy which shall be to all people. When members of Hierarchy consent to descend into form for the purpose of bringing truth to a world darkened by error, they stand as Messengers for the Most High God and for those who walk the invisible realms. Angels of Light are they, and they descend to mold the perfect will of God into the perfect will of man.

I come bearing the flame of obedience. For I have found that to build a nation, to build a destiny, and to complete the spiral of the Law, man must manifest obedience strict and stern to the sacrifice of all self and all selfishness, that the kingdom might reign and come into manifestation upon earth.

In my embodiment as George Washington, I was given the authority and the mission, as an emissary of the Brotherhood, to found a nation under Saint Germain, under God, that would be a home for all souls yearning to be obedient to the flame of freedom and to the flame of liberty. I am portrayed even today as having been stern, as having been a strong disciplinarian. I do not regret it, for this nation has waxed strong in greatness by those founding principles that were given into our consciousness and into our hands by the God of Freedom to the earth.

I remember well the rebellions of those who were not able to pass the test of the ten, and I knew it well as a test of discipleship and of understanding in the Law of Christ and His members. And when the Goddess of Liberty appeared to me as I knelt in prayer, she showed me not only the three great visions of the destiny of America, but also that he who would lead an army into battle must assume the responsibility of keeping the Flame of the Christ for each member of his troops. Not only did the great lady show me this, but she gave to me the impetus of her cosmic Threefold Flame to carry on in the tradition of the lovers of liberty, the sons and daughters of freedom, and the giants

SPIRITUAL WISDOM UNITING EAST AND WEST

Pearls of Wisdom are letters of instruction written each week by the Ascended Masters to their disciples throughout the world. They are sent on a love-offering basis to all who ask for them. The **Pearls of Wisdom** contain both fundamental and advanced teachings of the Great White Brotherhood, and they provide a wealth of material for inspired reading, practical application, and initiation on the path of self-mastery.

If you desire to be counted among the avant-garde of Light-bearers to humanity, take this opportunity to become better acquainted with the nature of the work and teachings of Hierarchy!

THE SUMMIT LIGHTHOUSE
Box A, Colorado Springs, CO 80901
Box 1227, Santa Barbara, CA 93102

A MESSAGE OF GENTLE ENFOLDING LOVE FROM LISTENING ANGEL

Book One of the Cherubim Library

A beautiful dictation by Listening Angel delivered in blank verse through the Messenger Mark L. Prophet. Delicately illustrated with thirteen reproductions from the engravings of Gustave Doré. A 48-page hardback printed in pink and blue on satin-shell paper. Ideal as a birthday or seasonal greeting to loved ones. $2.95 postpaid

THE SUMMIT LIGHTHOUSE
Box A, Colorado Springs, CO 80901
Box 1227, Santa Barbara, CA 93102

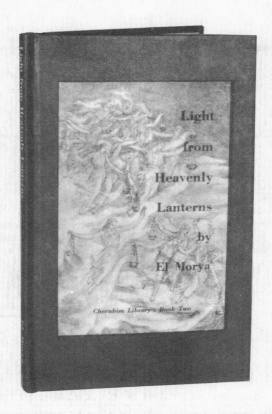

LIGHT FROM HEAVENLY LANTERNS
BY EL MORYA
Book Two of the Cherubim Library

A classic address of the Lord of the First Ray given through the Messenger Mark L. Prophet. Poetry and prose on the great flow of Life from God to man throughout Cosmos, together with a concise biography of El Morya's illustrious embodiments. This 42-page hardback printed in blue and violet on satin-shell paper is magnificently illustrated with ten drawings by Auriel Bessemer. A book to both keep and give away. $2.95 postpaid

THE SUMMIT LIGHTHOUSE
Box A, Colorado Springs, CO 80901
Box 1227, Santa Barbara, CA 93102

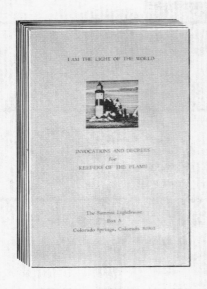

INVOCATIONS AND DECREES
FOR KEEPERS OF THE FLAME

An abundant selection of invocations, prayers, and decrees in prose and poetry for all who seek reunion with the Perfection of God. For daily meditation, self-transformation, and the healing of the nations. Color-coded to facilitate visualization of the Flames of the Holy Spirit. $4.50 postpaid

THE SUMMIT LIGHTHOUSE BOOK OF SONGS

Over 240 songs dedicated to the Christ, the I AM Presence, the Ascended Masters, Cosmic Beings, and angelic hosts. Words only. $4.50 postpaid

Both **Invocations and Decrees** and **Book of Songs** purchased as a set. $8.50 postpaid

THE SUMMIT LIGHTHOUSE
Box A, Colorado Springs, CO 80901
Box 1227, Santa Barbara, CA 93102

STUDIES OF THE HUMAN AURA
by Kuthumi

Twelve new manuscripts by the Master K. H., including several choice dictations by this well-known Brother of the Golden Robe, who writes from his retreat in Kashmir. Also included is a biographical sketch of his embodiments of devotion to the wisdom of the Christ.

In his penetrating study of this widely talked-about but little understood subject, Kuthumi will teach you the science of in-depth reading of the human aura and how to channel its unlimited power in the proper way.

Master the art of repelling negative auric emanations and protecting your consciousness from harmful projections! Experience the satisfaction of bringing out the special quality of beauty that is locked in your own aura until it becomes resplendent with Light and healing energies that can be used for the blessing of all Life!

This is your opportunity to step into the fourth dimension with a World Teacher who has brought thousands of disciples into cosmic realms of enlightenment and self-mastery. $2.95 postpaid

THE SUMMIT LIGHTHOUSE
Box A, Colorado Springs, CO 80901
Box 1227, Santa Barbara, CA 93102

THE OVERCOMING OF FEAR
THROUGH DECREES
by Lord Maitreya

An invaluable aid to understanding the science of decreeing. Table of Contents: Dictation by Lord Maitreya; The Power of the Spoken Word by Saint Germain; Heart, Head, and Hand Decrees by El Morya; The Power of the 10,000 times 10,000; How to Decree Effectively; Notes on the Color Rays from the Writings of Kuthumi; Helps to Effective Decreeing. 72-page paperback. $2.95 postpaid

THE SUMMIT LIGHTHOUSE
Box A, Colorado Springs, CO 80901
Box 1227, Santa Barbara, CA 93102